WALKING IN FREEDOM

MIKE RICHES

—— *A Companion to* ——

LIVING SET FREE IN CHRIST™

Walking in Freedom: A Companion to Living Set Free in Christ
Fifth Edition, January 2024
Copyright © 2024 SycPub Global, LLC

All rights reserved. No part of this publication may be reproduced, stored in a retrieval system, or transmitted in any form by any means, electronic, mechanical, photocopy, recording or otherwise, without the prior permission of the publisher, except as provided by USA copyright law.
1. You cannot make changes.
2. You cannot make copies without written permission from SycPub Global, LLC.
3. Additional books can be purchased from SycPub Global, LLC.

How to effectively use this material:
On behalf of all of us at SycPub Global, LLC, we pray this material will abundantly bless you, your family, and your church body. We want you to be free to share these biblical principles with friends and loved ones as God leads. However, we do ask that all use of this material be under the guidance of a trusted spiritual authority within your church body. This book is intended to be used in conjunction with the leading of an instructor in a classroom setting; it is not meant as a free-standing textbook. Also, we ask that you refrain from making photocopies without permission. Licenses to print are available on request. Thank you.

Unless otherwise noted, all Scripture quotations are taken from the Holy Bible, New Living Translation, © 1996. Used by permission of Tyndale House Publishers, Inc., Wheaton, Illinois 60189.

Scripture quotations marked (ESV) are from The Holy Bible, English Standard Version, © 2001 by Crossway Bibles, a division of Good News Publishers. Used by permission. All rights reserved.

Scriptures marked (NASV) are from the New American Standard Bible®, © 1960, 1962, 1963, 1968, 1971, 1972, 1973, 1975, 1977, 1995 by The Lockman Foundation. Used by permission. www.lockman.org.

Scripture quotations marked (NIV) are taken from the Holy Bible, New International Version®, NIV®. Copyright © 1973, 1978, 1984, 2011 by Biblica, Inc.™ Used by permission of Zondervan. All rights reserved worldwide.

Scriptures marked (NKJV) are from The New King James Version®, © 1982 by Thomas Nelson, Inc. Used by permission. All rights reserved.

Published by: SycPub Global, LLC
P.O. Box 158
Gig Harbor, WA 98335

To order: Website: www.sycpubglobal.org
Email: info@sycpubglobal.org

ISBN 978-1-7370261-0-5

Editorial and Book Packaging: Arlyn Lawrence, Inspira Literary Solutions, Gig Harbor, WA
Design: Brianna Showalter, Ruston, WA

CONTENTS

INTRODUCTION [5]

ANGER [6]
CONTROL [15]
CRITICAL SPIRIT [21]
ENTITLEMENTS [28]
FEAR [36]
HOPELESSNESS [44]
INSIGNIFICANCE & INFERIORITY [50]
JEALOUSY [57]
PASSIVITY [63]
PRIDE [71]
REBELLION [77]
REJECTION [84]
RELIGIOUS SPIRIT [92]
SELF-HATRED [101]
SHAME [108]
UNBELIEF [115]
UNFORGIVENESS [123]

ABOUT THE AUTHOR [132]

INTRODUCTION

It is for freedom that Christ has set us free (Galatians 5:1). Freedom is at the heart of the life and message of Jesus Christ and, therefore, His followers' mission. The *Walking in Freedom* course manual is designed to help you continue in your pursuit of "living set free."

The *Living Set Free* manual provides comprehensive teaching on living in the freedom in which God designed all of us to live. The *Walking in Freedom* material will help identify and practically apply spiritual transactions that result in freedom from particular bondages in your life. Through Christ's power and the simple steps in which you will be led, you can break out of specific bondages to live in the freedom Jesus purchased for you.

In this manual, you will find brief biblical insight on each stronghold. This teaching will be followed by diagnostic inventories that help identify if and how certain strongholds might exist in your life. You are then assisted in exercising spiritual transactions of freedom unique to each one. Every chapter then closes out with Scripture and declarations that help you walk in freedom.

You can use this manual on your own, with a partner, or with a small group. Allow the Holy Spirit to speak to you regarding how these strongholds might have been established in your life. You will undoubtedly be blessed and encouraged as you experience greater levels of freedom.

Keep in mind that experiencing freedom in any stronghold does not mean that you'll never have to face or deal with any of these issues again. What freedom does mean is that these strongholds will no longer control you. And you will become more proficient in using the divinely powerful weapons God has provided as you increase in your freedom.

Think of this as not merely going through a manual but as a developing lifestyle using divinely powerful weapons for a lifetime of freedom. Let the adventure begin!

ANGER

Anger is an emotion that involves a strong, uncomfortable, and hostile response to a perceived provocation, hurt or threat.

Anger destroys countless lives, for both those who live in anger and those who live as recipients of others' anger!

Most all of us have witnessed and lived under the tyrant of anger. It terrorizes, diminishes, and sometimes causes irreparable pain and damage in lives.

Everyday Health Media (https://www.everydayhealth.com/news/ways-anger-ruining-your-health) reports that studies reveal there are medical and health consequences of anger.

1. puts your heart at significant risk
2. raises potential for strokes
3. weakens your immune system
4. worsens anxiety
5. linked to depression
6. can hurt your lungs
7. can shorten your lifespan

The role anger plays in daily living is tragic. We see it in fractured marriages and divorce, domestic violence in spousal and child abuse, psychologically and emotionally damaged children due to the mismanaged anger of parents, tensions in the workplace, and people living in toxic relationships because of chronic anger.

Anger physically is a powerful emotion. When we are angry, sugar pours into our system, creating energy; blood pressure severely increases, our heart beats faster (up to 130 to 230 beats a minute), circulating needed increased nourishment, additional adrenalin is released, and muscles tense up.

Continuous anger can be harmful to one's body. Anger that is not released can keep a body in this charged state of rapid heartbeat, high blood pressure, blood chemical changes, and adrenalin rushes.

But more critical is the damage that anger does spiritually, emotionally, and relationally to one's life. The Bible warns us about anger; it must be dealt with biblically, otherwise it becomes a prime opportunity for Satan to do his work in our lives.

Anger can be difficult to recognize in ourselves. Anger is characterized as a *secondary emotion*, prompted by primary emotions or causes that typically leave one with hurt, fear, or frustration. Because anger has a powerful effect on one psychologically and physiologically, for many, it is a preferable emotion. But, anger as a lifestyle has serious side effects spiritually, emotionally, relationally, and physically.

There are many biblical accounts and admonitions concerning *anger*.

King Saul

King Saul was known for his anger, both godly and ungodly.

Holy Anger

In 1 Samuel 11, we read the account of a neighboring king of Ammon, King Nahash, was planning to humiliate and incapacitate a city in Israel—Jabesh Gilead. Israel had lived through a series of such onslaughts from neighboring kingdoms. Saul had just been anointed king of Israel. He received word of this new round of indignities, and verse 6 says:

> *Then the Spirit of God came powerfully upon Saul, and he became very angry.*

Ungodly Anger

Saul's anger seemed to erupt in ungodliness when David returned from battle, and the women greeted him with this song in 1 Samuel 18:7–8:

> *"Saul has slain his thousands, and David his ten thousands."* The Scriptures go on to tell us: *"Saul was very angry, and the saying displeased him."*

Saul twice threw his spear at David, trying to pin him to the wall (1 Sam. 18:10,11;19:9,10). He put David in a position of authority, hoping that he would fail to lead wisely and to discredit him.

Saul also required that David kill one hundred Philistines before he would give him his daughter in marriage, hoping that he would die while fighting the Philistines (1 Sam. 18:25–29).

Saul pursued David continually for more than a decade, forcing him to live in exile and frequently move from hiding place to hiding place (1 Sam. 24:26). He even turned on his son with murderous intent (see 1 Sam. 20:30). Saul's anger had no end.

Such outbursts of anger are easily recognizable, but just as damaging are the covert anger, the passive anger, which can reside in people.

Injustices

It is typical for strongholds in our lives to interface in active clusters. An example of this could be the group of *injustices, unforgiveness, and anger*.

It is most common for injustices to relate to one's anger. It typically shows itself in buried anger or deep sorrow over the past.

Injustice is *unmerited harm that came our way in the form of rejection and suffering*. We realize that we did nothing to deserve the treatment that was received, *and* that no recourse is available.

There are many biblical examples of injustices, such as Joseph in the Old Testament (Genesis 37–50). Jesus Himself suffered many injustices at the hands of people He created and came to redeem. Jesus' responses to His injustices were not ungodly. Therefore, the enemy could not find a place to exploit strongholds in His life.

Injustices can have a massive influence on our lives. Unknowingly our lives can labor under a cloud of lasting consequences from injustices. It is essential for each of us to address the accompanying tensions and emotions of the injustices we encounter.

Unforgiveness

We often live with unhealed wounds from injustices as a result of unforgiveness. Unforgiveness produces fruits of bitterness, anger, and rage, and opens the gates for all kinds of enemy strongholds to be in our lives. Loosed from the bondage that unforgiveness brings, we can heal, and the love of God can begin to flow out of our lives toward others.

The contrast of unforgiveness is "forgiveness." Forgiveness is the very foundation of God's Kingdom and the very nature of God Himself. Forgiveness is necessary when violated in one way or another, through injustice or otherwise. There is a debt to pay for restoration and healing to take place. The debt might be emotional, relational, financial, or physical; the debt might be the result of betrayal or related to our reputation. Regardless of the situation, a debt is owed to us.

To forgive, we must determine that we will release the offender (or the offending situation) from their obligation to us. We will not expect the offender to settle the debt. Such forgiveness is what Jesus did when He released us from having to pay the debt for the sins and violations we committed against Him. Forgiveness also is an exercise in faith—for we can only forgive in the context of real, God-like love and faith.

Exercising Faith in Forgiveness

- I will forgive others just like God has forgiven me.

- I will choose to confront issues, to offer forgiveness to the perpetrator(s), and leave the rest to God.

- I will grow more and more in understanding that the hurts of my past never escaped the eyes of the Lord.

- I will grow more and more in understanding that the hurts of my past are not to identify me or set the course of my future.

- I will not be kept in the bondage of unforgiveness.

- I will forgive others *regardless* of their response to me.

- I will allow others to see God's grace, mercy, and forgiveness in me!

- I will know and understand that forgiveness brings freedom and release from my past and present hurts.

Anger

It typically is understood that anger, in and of itself, is not a primary emotion or stronghold. Anger is a "secondary response," meaning that other issues lie underneath it to provoke and energize it. These matters can be wounds of injustice, betrayal, abandonment, and rejections. Also, anger is not only characterized as volcanic. It also can be passive. Others might not immediately or obviously recognize it. Passive anger is just buried and is no less dangerous than visible anger.

The cure for anger is forgiveness. It is essential first to understand and experience God's forgiveness of our sin. God chose to focus on His desire to forgive us rather than to hold us accountable for our failures (Psalm 103:12; Isaiah 43:25, 55:7).

Forgiveness demands payment. When someone has sinned against us and hurt us, our sense of justice requires that a fair payment be made. If that person cannot pay or chooses not to pay, either we resent the injustice and become bitter and angry, or we exercise forgiveness, leading to peace.

Forgiveness is not naturally easy, especially when something has caused us significant harm or damage. However, as we free the offender through forgiveness, we free ourselves. Keep in mind that one barometer indicating whether or not true forgiveness has occurred is our ability, through the Holy Spirit, to pray a blessing for a person who has hurt us.

DIAGNOSTICS OF ANGER

The following is a worksheet designed to assist you in approaching being set free from the bondage of anger. The first section aims to help you identify anger in your life. Mark the boxes that apply to prepare for working through the stronghold of anger.

- ❑ I feel relatively happy, and then I am struck with a sudden mood change.
- ❑ I can tend to raise my voice loudly and speak emphatically to make my point.
- ❑ I have an expressed impatience with others that often plays out in exasperation.
- ❑ I become angry when others "cannot read my mind." I want others to think just like I think, and be able to anticipate what I need.
- ❑ I become angry when not recognized for my contribution.
- ❑ I become angry when I feel I am disrespected, or when my words are not taken seriously.
- ❑ I know I am angry because of the language inside my head (cursing of myself or others).
- ❑ I know I am angry when I do not want to hear what another person has to say.
- ❑ I get angry when I do not have what I need.
- ❑ I get angry when people do not do what I say.
- ❑ I get angry when I cannot control a given situation.
- ❑ I get angry about suggestions that I have done something wrong.
- ❑ I get angry when I feel added pressure on my job, with finances, with personal responsibilities, and with expectations that are placed on me.
- ❑ I say I have forgiven, but I continue to reprocess those incidents in my mind.
- ❑ I look for opportunities to bring up old hurtful subjects.
- ❑ I find myself speaking negatively or critically of others.
- ❑ I easily become defensive.
- ❑ I quickly see the faults in others.
- ❑ I will see the proverbially half-filled glass as half empty.
- ❑ I get frustrated easily about the perceived faults and mistakes of others.
- ❑ I become impatient quickly.
- ❑ I feel like my life is harder than others. "I have been given a raw deal."

IDENTIFYING INJUSTICES AND UNFORGIVENESS IN YOUR LIFE

The next section is designed to help identify ways you might have received injustices and areas in which there is unforgiveness in your life. Some or all of these can contribute to a constant state of low-grade anger in your life, fits of anger, or even rage.

The following diagnostic is in regards to those closest to you, starting with your parents. Injustices at the most intimate level are most painful. Parents are where the greatest intimacy and trust should be found. Therefore, when there is hurt at this level, it is the most painful.

This kind of consideration should be given to all our relationships. The following is merely a diagnostic tool to help you identify potential sources of anger in your life. It also is not saying that your parents did not love you, try their best for you, or that you are disrespecting them.

Biological Dad/Step-Dad Or Mom/Step-Mom

Were the following elements present in your relationship? If a statement resonates with you, check the box. If it relates to your father, write "F" next to the box, and if it relates to your mother, write "M" next to the box.

- ☐ **Exasperation:** overuse of a wrong form of discipline that left you crushed in spirit and confused.
- ☐ **Control/manipulation**
- ☐ **The absence of spiritual leadership:** did your father demonstrate proactive spiritual leadership in your home?
- ☐ **Neglect:** did your dad spend purposeful time with you on a consistent basis; did he show interest in you and what was important to you?
- ☐ **Abandonment:** was your father absent spiritually, emotionally, mentally, and physically?
- ☐ **Rejection:** did you feel as though you were not fully accepted and embraced by your dad?
- ☐ **Passivity:** did your dad initiate relationship and direction in your life? Did he allow your mom to do what the Lord expected of her?
- ☐ **Criticism:** was your father critical of you or your abilities?
- ☐ **Performance-based acceptance and love:** were you rewarded with words of encouragement only when you measured up to specific expectations of your dad?
- ☐ **Alcohol abuse:** did it have an adverse and damaging effect on your family environment and you?
- ☐ **Drug use:** did it cause an adverse and harmful effect on your family environment and you?
- ☐ **Pornography**
- ☐ **Adultery**
- ☐ **Divorce**
- ☐ **Physical abuse**
- ☐ **Emotional abuse**
- ☐ **Sexual abuse**

The following sins of <u>omission</u> are things that your father did not do. Often these sins are just as or more damaging than sins of commission.

- **Withholding affection:** did your dad demonstrate strong, manly affection toward you and your family or was it sterile of warmth in displayed fondness?
- **Withholding blessing:** did your dad speak words of life, destiny, hope, and blessing into your life?
- **Withholding words of encouragement:** did your dad recognize your times of discouragement or difficulty and initiate words of encouragement?
- **Withholding discipline:** did your dad provide you the security of well-defined boundaries and help build discipline in your life?
- **Were your brothers or sisters treated in a way that left you bitter?**
- **Was either of your parents treated in a way that left you bitter?**

THE 4 Rs FOR ANGER

REPENTANCE

Grant Forgiveness:

Sample Prayer: Lord Jesus, I forgive my dad/mom for the sin of _____.
(List here the sins for which you need to forgive your dad and or mom and go through them one at a time. It is important to recognize how these injustices against you made you feel. It is then essential that you grant forgiveness for that consequence.)

Sample Prayer: Lord Jesus, I forgive my dad/mom for the sin of _____.
(List here the sins for which you need to forgive your dad or mom and go through them one at a time. It is important to recognize how these injustices affected you spiritually, emotionally, mentally, volitionally, and physically. It is then essential that you grant forgiveness for each consequence.)

Ask Forgiveness:

Sample Prayer: *Lord, I ask You to forgive me for the sin of unforgiveness toward my mom and/or dad related to these injustices. I am sorry for any bitterness and resentment toward them. I also ask Your forgiveness for my rebellion. Finally, I ask forgiveness for my anger. I break all curses, negative thoughts, or slander I have spoken. I replace those curses now with blessings!*

Bless: *(with conviction.)*

Sample Prayer: *Lord, I bless my father and my mother with _____.* (If they are no longer living, bless their memory as if they were physically in front of you. This will be for your benefit.) The following are some suggestions, but let God's Spirit direct you.

- bless with salvation
- bless with the same freedom I have found today
- bless with a new and soft heart
- bless the marriage
- bless finances and work
- bless with joy, peace, kindness, love, and all of the fruit of the Spirit
- bless with a long life and with excellent health
- bless for being a father who provided me with food, clothing, and shelter
- other . . .

Father, I declare that I love my mom and dad; I look at each through Your eyes. Thank You for the power of the Cross.

REBUKE

(Pray the following prayer with conviction and in faith that God will move powerfully right now.)

Sample Prayer: *I rebuke and bind the lies of the enemy right now and their attack on my life in the area of anger. I rebuke the spirits of rejection, abandonment, unforgiveness, resentment, and anger. I command you to the feet of Jesus to receive your judgment.*

REPLACE

Sample Prayer: *Lord, I replace my right to see justice with the Spirit of Christ in forgiveness. I will live in a spirit of forgiveness, forbearance, grace and mercy, and security in Jesus. I will not live in anger and resentment, but instead, I will live generously toward others regarding forgiveness in mercy, grace, and forbearance.*

RECEIVE

Request the empowering of the Holy Spirit to fill every place previously inhabited by the sin of anger fueled by unforgiveness. Thank the Lord that He has forgiven you. Receive His full cleansing and rejoice.

Sample Prayer: *Fill me with Your Holy Spirit that I may live supernaturally in the freedom of forgiveness and trust in You in faith. Lord, I receive Your forgiveness for the sin of anger in my life. I receive Your love for me.*

WALKING IN THE OPPOSITE SPIRIT

- ☐ I will forgive.
- ☐ I will serve.
- ☐ I will exercise gratitude.
- ☐ I control any anger so that it serves a godly purpose and not a destructive one.
- ☐ I will not go to bed angry.
- ☐ I will be prayerful and patient instead of angry.
- ☐ I will repay evil with good and, where needed, love those who have made me their enemy.
- ☐ God's love will control me.
- ☐ I will live out the fruit of the Spirit (love, joy, peace, forbearance, kindness, goodness, faithfulness, gentleness, and self-control).

SCRIPTURES

***Proverbs 19:11** (NLT)*
Sensible people control their temper; they earn respect by overlooking wrongs.

***Ecclesiastes 7:8–9** (NLT)*
Finishing is better than starting. Patience is better than pride. Control your temper, for anger labels you a fool.

***Romans 12:12** (NIV)*
Be joyful in hope, patient in affliction, faithful in prayer.

***Ephesians 4:26–27** (NLT)*
And "don't sin by letting anger control you." Don't let the sun go down while you are still angry, for anger gives a foothold to the devil.

***1 Thessalonians 5:14** (NIV)*
And we urge you, brothers and sisters, warn those who are idle and disruptive, encourage the disheartened, help the weak, be patient with everyone.

***1 Peter 4:8** (NIV)*
Above all, love each other deeply, because love covers over a multitude of sins.

CONTROL

Control: *A strong need and determination to manipulate and manage one's own environment, life, situations, people, and circumstances, resulting in frustration, fear, insecurity, or anger when unable to do so.*

God's Design Gone Wrong: God designed humans with the capacity to lead, manage, and steward. It is part of our original design as humans created in God's image to take the initiative, be directive, and have godly influence over things, situations, and people. However, when those godly qualities become corrupted, "godly influence" can turn into imposing one's will upon others and situations. Such characteristics are an indication of a spirit (or stronghold) of *control.*

The Root of Control: Anxiety almost always fuels this need to control; at the heart of this stronghold of control there typically will be a corresponding fear (e.g., fear of failure, fear of rejection or abandonment, fear of betrayal or being hurt, fear of chaos, etc.). Insecurity also contributes to a controlling mindset and behavior.

Control also can be the response to having suffered hurts, injustices, and betrayals in life. Such experiences are painful and cause a person not to trust others. To hopefully preempt such experiences happening again there is an effort to control individuals and circumstances.

Being "in control" gives the temporary illusion of peace and security in the face of those fears. But unhealthy expressions of control are debilitating to you and others. Control also diminishes and frustrates those around you—hindering growth, dividing relationships, and stunting creativity.

The Development of Unhealthy Control: Many times the stronghold of control is established early in life, so soon that people mistakenly think it is part of their personality rather than a sin and an ungodly corruption of their original design. This stronghold characterizes itself by perfectionism, orderliness, workaholic tendencies, making one's self indispensable, having an inability to trust others, difficulty in delegating to or empowering others, and a fear of having personal flaws exposed. Deep down, people operating out of a stronghold of control resist being vulnerable. They believe they can protect themselves by staying in control of every aspect of their lives.

Our identity and our emotions can be immersed in the stronghold of control. There are few, if any, emotions related to control; feelings typically come when we feel <u>out</u> of control and that we must, therefore, <u>take</u> control. The process by which control establishes itself can be extremely subtle. People who live with it seldom notice it in themselves.

A Biblical Example of Control: We note King Saul (1 Sam. 14 and 19) again. His control brought confusion, discouragement, and defeat to his army and family. He wanted to secure himself, his position, his reputation, and his kingdom. In doing so, he put his army at risk, threatened the life of his faithful son Jonathan, and attempted to take the life of his loyal servant David.

King Saul's fears, insecurities, and jealousies, which he tried to compensate for through control, eventually alienated from him his family, his confidants, his subjects, and his soldiers. Various levels of relational, emotional, and physical alienation and isolation will characterize relationships with people who are controlling.

Does the stronghold of control evidence itself in your life? Prayerfully consider the following list and check any that apply to you:

Control through Communication

- ❏ I can tend to communicate disapproval (verbally or non-verbally) with the aim of changing other people.
- ❏ I will tend not to disclose complete information but only disclose information which I think will serve my purposes.
- ❏ I will speak and act in such a way as to put myself in a better light or to fulfill my desires.
- ❏ I tend to want to control information and the communicating of information within a group.

Relational Control:

- ❏ I passively or actively dominate conversations.
- ❏ I will "take charge."
- ❏ I feel I know what is best for other people.
- ❏ I tend to make other people work around me.

- ❏ I resist having others speak openly into my life.
- ❏ I fear being hurt or rejected by others.
- ❏ I find it difficult to encourage, empower, and release others.
- ❏ If someone does not want to do what I want them to do, I become more persuasive until they agree.
- ❏ When I don't receive the response I desire immediately, I continue to press for it.

Mindsets of Control:

- ❏ I am easily frustrated by changes in plans.
- ❏ I think my way of doing things is always the best.
- ❏ I tend to do things for others, usually because I think I can do it better than they can.
- ❏ I have a hard time accepting the opinions of others.
- ❏ I try to take control of situations when I am uncomfortable or when things are not going my way.
- ❏ I am often nervous when someone else is in control, and I am not.
- ❏ I feel it is my responsibility to help others understand and "get better."
- ❏ I am upset by group activities or projects in which others do not perform to my standards.
- ❏ When people don't follow my suggestions or do what I think is best, I feel rejected or angry.
- ❏ I think I am the best one to manage most situations and feel frustrated when others don't respect my abilities and wisdom.
- ❏ I tend to feel uncomfortable and distrusting when put in a new situation or when I encounter unfamiliar circumstances.
- ❏ I find it difficult to follow others.
- ❏ I try to gain pity or sympathy from others.
- ❏ I think my way of doing things is the best.
- ❏ I desire recognition.
- ❏ I usually know best.
- ❏ I always have an answer to justify my stance or my situation.
- ❏ I am afraid of being wrong, so I will push a subject until others give in.

THE 4 Rs FOR CONTROL

REPENTANCE

Take responsibility for control by confessing specifically the sin of trusting in yourself instead of resting in the Lord. Often there is need to forgive people and or institutions from which you have suffered injustices, love deficits, and or betrayal. Forgive the responsible individuals for what happened to you, and what it did to you.

Then confess any anger, pride, frustration, or fear you have had that is related to your control.

> **Sample Prayer:** *Lord, I forgive the persons (name them), what they did to me (identify the actions and events) and what it has done to me (name the specific emotional, spiritual, physical, and practical consequences).*
>
> *I repent of the sin of control and manipulation. I confess right now that I have allowed it to become a part of my life. I call it out before You as sin. I confess wanting control over others and my own life. I break control in any area of my life right now by turning in the opposite direction and living a life of trust in and yielding to You, Your Word, and Your ways.*

REBUKE

Renounce every lie you have held onto concerning your need or ability to control the people and situations in your life. In the authority of Jesus Christ, resist Satan and any evil spirits that have found a place to oppress you through arrogance, frustration, and fear over lack of control.

> **Sample Prayer:** *I rebuke and bind the lies of the enemy right now. Their attack on my life in the area of control is broken. I refuse to believe that God does not have control over every situation. I renounce the lie that I am the master of my fate. I sever all ties to the stronghold of control. I rebuke every evil spirit that has empowered the stronghold of control in my life. I command you to the feet of Jesus to receive His judgment for you.*

REPLACE

It takes an absolute hatred for the sin of control in order to walk free of it. It is a deep cleansing in your personality, including your ways of thinking, your reactions, and your motives. When you begin to feel internal angst, stop and ask the Lord if control is the issue. If it is, confess it and receive His cleansing.

Acknowledge and affirm that God is the only One worthy of controlling your life and that His plans for you are perfect in every way.

> **Sample Prayer:** *I right now declare by God's grace that I will live in such a way as to trust God with my life. I trust Him with my well-being and my future. I will not try to control others but instead, trust and empower others. I will live for their benefit and well-being, believing that God is doing the same for me.*

RECEIVE

Request and receive the filling of the Holy Spirit to fill every place that was once inhabited by the sin of control. Thank the Lord that He has forgiven you. Receive His full cleansing and rejoice.

> **Sample Prayer:** *Lord, fill me with Your Holy Spirit that I may live supernaturally in the freedom of faith, trust in You, and serving others. I receive Your forgiveness for the sin of control in my life. I receive Your love for me.*

WALKING IN THE OPPOSITE SPIRIT

- [ ] Jesus never controlled people but allowed them to respond by their own free will.
- [ ] Jesus allowed His disciples to make mistakes and go out on mission.
- [ ] The father of the prodigal son (Luke 15) allowed the son to leave and face the consequences of his poor choices.
- [ ] Whereas control hinders growth, divides relationships, and stunts creativity, freedom stimulates growth, unity, creativity, and power.
- [ ] Father, You are Lord of my life and every situation; control belongs to You alone.
- [ ] I want to trust in You with all my heart, and so I release control of the people in my life—my family, friends, and co-workers—to You, who alone knows what is best.
- [ ] I replace manipulating situations and people with quiet trust in Your goodness and faithfulness.
- [ ] I walk in the opposite spirit of control, which is that of submissive service to others.
- [ ] I replace the pride of thinking I know what is best for me with the humility of receiving spiritual input into my life from others.
- [ ] I replace the arrogance of not depending on others with a childlike trust in God's kindness to me through the members of His body.
- [ ] I replace anger, frustration, irritation, and fear over lack of control with unceasing prayer over the needs I face.
- [ ] The enemy would love nothing more than to destroy God's plan for your life. It takes an absolute hatred for the sin of control to walk free of it. It is a deep cleansing in your personality, including your ways of thinking, your reactions, and your motives.
- [ ] The opposite of control is serving. Affirm God's love for each of us and ask Him to deepen your understanding of others so as to regard and serve them in a Christlike manner.

SCRIPTURES:

Psalm 37:5
Commit your way to the Lord, trust also in Him, and He will do it.

Proverbs 3:5–6
Trust in the Lord with all of your heart and do not lean on your own understanding. In all your ways acknowledge Him, and He will make your paths straight.

Matthew 6:32–33
But seek first His kingdom and His righteousness, and all these things will be added to you. So do not worry about tomorrow, for tomorrow will care for itself. Each day has enough trouble of its own.

James 4:14–17
Come now, you who say "Today or tomorrow we will go to such and such a city, and spend a year there and engage in business and make a profit." Yet you do not know what your life will be like tomorrow. You are just a vapor that appears for a little while and then vanishes away. Instead, you ought to say, "If the Lord wills, we will live and also do this or that." But as it is, you boast in your arrogance; all such boasting is evil.

NOTES:

> **Criticism** is "an act of criticizing; to judge as a critic; to find fault; to blame or condemn."
>
> A **"critical spirit"** is an obsessive attitude of criticism and fault-finding, which seeks to tear down rather than build up.

A critical spirit regards people and circumstances from a negative point of view. It is pessimistic, impatient, irritable, unforgiving, unbending, and ungrateful toward others.

A critical spirit is the opposite of a positive, optimistic, and enthusiastic perspective and attitude.

An Example

The first generation of Israelites coming out of Egypt would have been characterized as having a critical spirit. Everything was negative in their view. They were critical of everything God and Moses in obedience to God did. And it was epidemic. One of the first examples is found in Genesis 14 as they stand on the shores of the Red Sea in their exodus out of Egypt.

> *Exodus 14:11–12 (ESV) They said to Moses, "Is it because there are no graves in Egypt that you have taken us away to die in the wilderness? What have you done to us in bringing us out of Egypt? Is not this what we said to you in Egypt: 'Leave us alone that we may serve the Egyptians?' For it would have been better for us to serve the Egyptians than to die in the wilderness."*

These verses are just the tip of the iceberg in terms of their critical spirit. It was incessant. It produced negativity, discouragement, unbelief, disobedience, and rebellion. God had mercy on them in this instance. But eventually, God had no choice but to judge them, and on several occasions.

Many suffered affliction, loss, disease, plagues, and even death. Instead of moving forward into blessing and a good land, they had to wander in a desert and wilderness. Where a critical spirit pervades faith, hope, and love cannot. God's power and favor cannot be unleashed in such an environment.

A Practical Look at the Critical Spirit

Everybody suffers in a culture of a critical spirit. A critical spirit dwells on the negative, looking for flaws rather than positive qualities in others. People operating in this stronghold are constantly complaining or criticizing and usually upset with something or somebody. They often have little control over their tongue or their temper and have tendencies for gossip, slander, strife, and malice.

A critical spirit can be very detrimental and damaging to a person's personal faith and to the health and vitality of a family or any group. Over time, if left unchecked, it prevents people from seeing, appreciating, and enjoying all that's truly good in the world—all that God is actively doing.

The critical person comes to expect, even to hope, that everything will have something wrong with it. Taken to the extreme, a critical person can assume the role of the "devil's advocate." One's very identity can be marked by this "need" for negativity. But critical people aren't just hurting themselves; they are also negatively affecting others as well.

The Roots of a Critical Spirit

Sometimes a critical spirit results from growing up in a culture/environment where criticism flowed from those held captive by pride, arrogance, or living as victims.

Sometimes a person becomes critical in response to an offense or because of a decision to live in response to an injustice against them. It is important to identify the root cause so the person can grant forgiveness and blessing to the offending person or situation, and then the 4Rs should be applied.

Factors in a Critical Spirit

1. **Our sinful or selfish nature** is referred to in the Bible as "the flesh." A critical person is *walking in the flesh*, not the Spirit. Cynicism inhibits faith and quenches the Spirit of God, causing them to live based on negative feelings, not faith. Godly people will always be optimistic and full of hope because they know, love, and serve a good, great, and gracious God.

2. **Poor self-image** It's been said, "Hurting people hurt people." This is demonstrably true. When you meet people who are constantly critical, you can be pretty sure that they're suffering from a poor self-image.

3. **Insecurity.** Criticism is often a conscious or subconscious means to elevate one's own self-esteem or self-image. By putting others down, these people are inwardly trying to build themselves up by attempting to feel more important or appearing more knowledgeable.

4. **Immaturity** denotes being childlike in behavior. Such a posture looks for someone to blame for problems and tends to be self-absorbed. An immature person is not comfortable with themselves and tends to seek validation through diminishing others.

5. **An unrenewed mind.** Paul says that our thinking and attitude should be regularly renewed by God's Word, which teaches us to bear the infirmities of the weak, to love, show compassion and offer encouragement. (see Eph. 4:23).

6. **A root of bitterness** develops when we fail to obtain the grace of God to forgive. When we fail to forgive others, we become angry, bitter, and resentful—not better.

7. **Bad company.** The reality is, for better or worse, we become like those with whom we associate. Paul says in 1 Corinthians 15:33, that we should not be deceived; bad company ruins good morals or corrupts good character.

8. **The devil** specializes in influencing negative, obsessive, sinful attitudes and behavior. He may use any of these factors or other techniques to influence a complaining or critical attitude and to stir up turmoil and strife within the Body of Christ.

The Fruits of a Critical Spirit

- creating a negative, sour, judgmental, and repressive atmosphere

- pointing out the weaknesses, idiosyncrasies, and inconsistencies of others with a view to tearing them down instead of building them up

- criticizing family, friends, co-workers, and members of the church family without bringing solutions, encouragement, or positive motivation

- quenching vision, creativity, unity, and teamwork

- reinforcing patterns of impatience, intolerance, and rigidity

- demoralizing people and creating a platform for rejection (children are especially vulnerable to this influence, and may pick up rejection that remains with them the rest of their lives).

DIAGNOSING A CRITICAL SPIRIT

- ❑ I am impatient with others' weaknesses.
- ❑ I am hard on those closest to me.
- ❑ I am much more likely to be rigid and unyielding than flexible and considerate.
- ❑ I am intolerant of people who are different from me or who fail to measure up to my standards.
- ❑ I have high expectations of other people, ministries, organizations, businesses, and institutions; I feel and/or demonstrate anger when those expectations are not met.
- ❑ I have a tendency to carry a grudge and I harbor resentment when I am wronged.
- ❑ I take it on myself to feel offended for others when I feel they have been wronged.
- ❑ I retaliate against people who have offended me or with whom I disagree; I use cutting words when I talk with them or I talk behind their backs; I avoid them.
- ❑ I feel a need to draw attention to the shortcomings of others (e.g., family and friends, members of my small group or my church) in the hope of persuading them to my point of view.
- ❑ I disguise my negative and critical spirit with statements like, *"I am discerning,"* or *"I am just being realistic,"* or, *"Let's be real about this."*
- ❑ I think less of others whose standards differ from mine on issues of Christian liberty.
- ❑ I cannot honor, fellowship with, or minister freely with other Christians whose theological views, worship styles, or ministry practices are different from mine.
- ❑ I resist change; I have difficulty considering new ideas and new ways of doing things.

THE 4 Rs FOR CRITICAL SPIRIT

We must confess and repent of any and all attitudes and actions related to a critical spirit. We must rebuke and renounce the lies and influences surrounding it, and we must replace it with a spirit of forbearing grace by continually renewing our minds with God's Word. We also must faithfully seek, receive, and depend on the power of the Holy Spirit to enable us to walk continuously in the truth. Use this worksheet as a guide, and walk through the 4Rs:

REPENTANCE

Take responsibility for your critical spirit by confessing it as sin.

Often there is a need to forgive people and or institutions from which you have suffered injustices, love deficits, and or betrayal. Forgive them for what happened and what it did to you.

Then confess any anger, pride, bitterness, or resentment that you have had related to your critical spirit.

> **Sample Prayer:** *Lord, I forgive the persons (name them), what they did to me (identify the actions and events) and what it has done to me (name the specific emotional, spiritual, physical, and practical consequences).*
>
> *I repent of my sin of a critical spirit. I confess right now that I have allowed it to become a part of my life. I call it out before You as sin. I confess to being critical over others and situations. I confess my sin of pride and arrogance, and thinking I am better than others, and that I have the right to be the judge. I break this critical spirit off of my life right now by turning in the opposite direction and living a life that is positive, faith-filled, encouraging, and a blessing to others.*

REBUKE

Renounce every lie you have held onto concerning your need or that is negative or critical of people and situations in your life. In the authority of Jesus Christ, resist Satan and any evil spirits that have found an open door to empower criticism in your life.

> **Sample Prayer:** *I rebuke and bind the lies of the enemy right now. Their attack on my life in the area of being negative and critical is broken. I refuse to believe that God does not have control over every situation. I renounce the lie that I am better than others, that I have the right to be judge. I sever all ties to the stronghold of a critical spirit. I rebuke every evil spirit that has empowered the stronghold of a critical spirit in my life. I command you to the feet of Jesus to receive His judgment for you.*

REPLACE

It takes an absolute hatred for the sin of a critical spirit in order to walk free of it. It is a deep cleansing of part of your personality, including your ways of thinking, your reactions, and your motives. When you begin to feel critical and negative, stop, repent, and pray or speak blessing over the person or situation. Determine to live out Ephesians 4:29 so that only words and attitudes that build up others come from you.

> **Sample Prayer:** *I right now declare by God's grace that I will live in such a way as to be positive, faith-filled, encouraging, and a blessing to others and every situation in which I am a part. I trust God with my well-being and my future. I will trust and empower others. I will live for their benefit and well-being, trusting that God is doing the same for me.*

RECEIVE

Request and receive the filling of the Holy Spirit to fill every place that was once inhabited by the sin of a critical spirit. Thank the Lord that He has totally forgiven you. Receive His full cleansing and rejoice.

Sample Prayer: *Lord, Fill me with Your Holy Spirit that I may live supernaturally in the freedom of faith and trust in You and to serve others. I receive Your forgiveness and I receive Your love for me.*

WALKING IN THE OPPOSITE SPIRIT

Cultivate the following virtues of forbearing grace—the opposite of a critical spirit—in your life:

- ❏ I will be patient and forbearing toward the weaknesses of others.
- ❏ I will guard myself against speaking harshly or critically to my spouse and my children.
- ❏ I will not take or carry offenses for myself or for others.
- ❏ When there is a need to discuss differences, I will communicate in humility and speak the truth in love.
- ❏ I will offer my opinions only when asked, or under the direction of the Holy Spirit.
- ❏ I will trust God to lead those in authority over me, give them my support and cooperation, and extend unlimited grace to them when needed.
- ❏ I will lead others in an understanding and patient manner.
- ❏ I will look for practical ways to compensate for the weaknesses of others.
- ❏ When someone accuses or criticizes me, I will respond with humility and an open mind; I will not respond defensively.
- ❏ When I feel I am being attacked personally by someone, I will choose to look at the situation through spiritual eyes, being on the alert for schemes of the enemy.
- ❏ I will be vigilant in guarding both my marriage and my children from any critical spirits in our midst.
- ❏ I will make it a high priority to work to preserve unity in my family, with my friends, in my church, with other Christians, and with those others God brings into my life.

SCRIPTURES:

Job 16:4–5 (NLT) *I could say the same things if you were in my place. I could spout off my criticisms against you and shake my head at you. But that's not what I would do. I would speak in a way that helps you. I would try to take away your grief.*

Proverbs 17:9 *He who covers over an offense promotes love, but whoever repeats the matter separates close friends.*

Matthew 7:1–2 *"Do not judge, or you too will be judged. For in the same way you judge others, you will be judged, and with the measure you use, it will be measured to you."*

Matthew 7:3–5 *"Why do you look at the speck of sawdust in your brother's eye and pay no attention to the plank in your own eye? How can you say to your brother, 'Let me take the speck out of your eye,' when all the time there is a plank in your own eye? You hypocrite, first take the plank out of your own eye, and then you will see clearly to remove the speck from your brother's eye."*

Luke 6:37 *"Do not judge, and you will not be judged. Do not condemn, and you will not be condemned. Forgive, and you will be forgiven."*

Romans 14:10–13 *You, then, why do you judge your brother? Or why do you look down on your brother? For we will all stand before God's judgment seat. It is written: "As surely as I live," says the Lord, "every knee will bow before me; every tongue will confess to God." So then, each of us will give an account of himself to God. Therefore let us stop passing judgment on one another. Instead, make up your mind not to put any stumbling block or obstacle in your brother's way*

Galatians 6:1–4 *Brothers, if someone is caught in a sin, you who are spiritual should restore him gently. But watch yourself, or you also may be tempted. Carry each other's burdens, and in this way you will fulfill the law of Christ. If anyone thinks he is something when he is nothing, he deceives himself. Each one should test his own actions. Then he can take pride in himself, without comparing himself to somebody else.*

Colossians 3:13–14 *Bear with each other and forgive whatever grievances you may have against one another. Forgive as the Lord forgave you. And over all these virtues put on love, which binds them all together in perfect unity.*

James 2:12–13 *Speak and act as those who are going to be judged by the law that gives freedom, because judgment without mercy will be shown to anyone who has not been merciful. Mercy triumphs over judgment!*

James 4:11–12 *Brothers, do not slander one another. Anyone who speaks against his brother or judges him speaks against the law and judges it. When you judge the law, you are not keeping it, but sitting in judgment on it. There is only one Lawgiver and Judge, the one who is able to save and destroy. But you - who are you to judge your neighbor?*

ENTITLEMENTS

An entitlement is a state or condition of living with rights or conditions; it is a belief that one is deserving of or has a right to certain privileges.

The term "entitlement culture" has been used to describe America. We also are described as living in an age of expectations. This reality makes it more challenging to identify entitlements because our standard as to how we regard entitlements is different than other cultures in the world and most definitely different than the biblical standard.

Entitlement's True Issue: The central issue of entitlements is that we put limits on what God can ask of us. We are saying, "Yes Lord, but…" and then the conditions within which we will or will not give ourselves to God in obedience or service come forth.

Biblical Example

Jesus is the ultimate model of one who not only refused to live with entitlements but who generously lived as a servant in obedience to God, to advance God's Kingdom in people's lives, and to serve others. Paul states this in his letter to the Philippians:

> *Philippians 2:5–8 (NLT) You must have the same attitude that Christ Jesus had. Though he was God, he did not think of equality with God as something to cling to. Instead, he gave up his divine privileges; he took the humble position of a **slave** and was born as a human being. When he appeared in human form, he humbled himself in obedience to God and died a criminal's death on a cross.*

A slave [*doulos*—"doo·los"] is one who is in a permanent relation of servitude to another; his or her will is being altogether consumed in the will of the other. Jesus took on the posture of a slave. Jesus gave Himself up to another's will, His Father's. Jesus gave up His interests to extend and advance God's cause among humanity.

Our attitude should be the same as that of Jesus Christ (Philippians 2:5). As Jesus considered himself "of no reputation" and poured Himself out for us (no entitlements), we are called to do the same. We are to lay down our entitlements, along with the attitudes and actions that come from them so that we may take up the same mindset as Christ Jesus.

In the Gospels, we read that many people approached Jesus to follow Him, but came with entitlements or conditions. The entitlements were diverse, but Jesus' response was the same each time.

> *Matthew 8:21–22 (NLT) Another of his disciples said, "Lord, first let me return home and bury my father." But Jesus told him, "Follow me now. Let the spiritually dead bury their own dead."*
>
> *Matthew 10:37 (NLT) "If you love your father or mother more than you love me, you are not worthy of being mine; or if you love your son or daughter more than me, you are not worthy of being mine."*
>
> *Matthew 16:24 (NLT) Then Jesus said to his disciples, "If any of you wants to be my follower, you must turn from your selfish ways, take up your cross, and follow me."*

Entitlement's Spiritual Essence

Entitlements ultimately put us in bondage. More critically, they limit how God can use us. God's presence, power, and Kingdom outcomes are restricted according to the entitlements with which we live.

DIAGNOSTIC QUESTIONS

Please check any boxes that you believe may apply to you. If the Lord reveals to you entitlements not listed, write them down. Begin by praying for God's Spirit to give you personal revelation in this exercise as to entitlements in your life. Then use your diagnostic work as a guide to work through your spiritual transactions using the 4 Rs, which follow.

1. **Time.** This directly conflicts with the Lord's desire for us to relinquish our time completely to Him. "All of me for the sake of others" is the heart cry of a servant. Time entitlements limit what the Lord can ask of me as I maintain control of my time. (There are fundamental needs for rest, rejuvenation, relational time for your family, etc.; these are not at issue here.)

    My entitlement to:
    - ❏ put first my own and my family's desires (not essential needs) over ministry/Kingdom mission and serving others
    - ❏ be able to do what I want in my free time, versus asking God what He wants me to do
    - ❏ my routine
    - ❏ my down time
    - ❏ _____
    - ❏ _____

2. **Comforts.** Comfort entitlements have to do with things we think our flesh needs to be happy or content. They can include food, entertainment, buying things, etc. The key is to identify what we "want" for our own comfort and desire at the expense of God's purposes in and through us.

   My entitlement to:
   - ☐ withdraw when I am uncomfortable
   - ☐ have my desires met
   - ☐ enjoy a certain standard of living
   - ☐ work only with people and in settings that are comfortable to me
   - ☐ people understanding me
   - ☐ _____
   - ☐ _____

3. **Money.** Money entitlements create expectations that I will have a certain standard of living, often based upon social standing and a false identity. Money entitlements and comfort entitlements are closely related.

   My entitlement to:
   - ☐ have the best of everything
   - ☐ reward myself by spending money
   - ☐ a financial cushion
   - ☐ control of my finances
   - ☐ first secure my own future
   - ☐ give to God what is His out of my surplus and comfort
   - ☐ keep my property and possessions to myself
   - ☐ _____
   - ☐ _____

4. **Appearance.** Appearance entitlement says I must meet a certain standard for how I appear. The focus is on the outward approval of man, rather than approval from simple and complete obedience to God.

   My entitlement to:
   - ❑ position/status/title
   - ❑ have people respect me
   - ❑ dress the way I want; disregard others
   - ❑ have my family and kids enjoy the privileges and standards of our culture
   - ❑ non-essential things like new clothes or eating out because I feel I deserve them
   - ❑ _____
   - ❑ _____

5. **Recognition and reward.** Others must recognize what I have done. This entitlement demands that others "notice" my service and acknowledge it. I become offended when I am not acknowledged. Or my entitlement asks for some kind of compensation for obedience and service, as if obedience is beyond the call of duty. Rewards come in many forms. There's only one response called for, and that is, "Yes!" from the heart. God will not be indebted to any person.

   My entitlement to:
   - ❑ remain hidden
   - ❑ have others pay attention to me
   - ❑ be treated fairly always
   - ❑ have a respected position/title/role
   - ❑ be supported and affirmed
   - ❑ be called on, have an inside track on what is happening
   - ❑ affirmation or credit when I do something for God or others
   - ❑ _____
   - ❑ _____

6. **Conditions for service.** I want to determine whether I will serve, where and whom I will serve. This is not based on the Lord's direction, but on my own likes and dislikes. I put limits on what the Lord can ask of me. I want to be in control.

   My entitlement to:
   - ❑ understand; things must first be very clear or spelled out
   - ❑ serve where I want
   - ❑ know what others know
   - ❑ do it my way

- ☐ control timing
- ☐ not suffer
- ☐ decide for myself (independence vs. interdependence)
- ☐ have what others have (seat of jealousy)
- ☐ use gifts as I think they should be used
- ☐ my opinions being heard
- ☐ my needs met by others
- ☐ be understood
- ☐ God answering prayer the way I feel He should
- ☐ have others meet my standards
- ☐ _____
- ☐ _____

7. **Emotions.** "But this is how I feel!" My emotions legitimize my disobedience. "I have a right to be angry and resentful because I feel . . .!" Emotions are <u>not</u> an excuse to sin and selfishness.

    My entitlement to hold onto:
    - ☐ sorrow
    - ☐ anger
    - ☐ victimization
    - ☐ inferiority/inadequacy
    - ☐ unforgiveness/resentment
    - ☐ exceptionalism
    - ☐ fear
    - ☐ complacency
    - ☐ being critical
    - ☐ hurts and wounds of the past to excuse me from responsibility and service today
    - ☐ _____
    - ☐ _____

We need only get revelation of our entitlements and get moving on the path to destroy them. Ask the Lord—right now—to reveal all areas of entitlements. Tell Him that you will attack these areas in obedience and dependent on His grace.

THE 4 Rs FOR ENTITLEMENTS

REPENTANCE

To repent, you must admit the specific things to which you feel you have rights, or that you deserve. When we choose to follow Christ, we yield to Him all our rights. Confess any specific sense of entitlement you might, such as getting people to do what you want, expectations that you should get what you want from God or others, or a sense of entitlement that you can manage your own life and time.

> **Sample Prayer:** *Lord, I repent of the sin of entitlement, of wanting to have my own way and expecting that You and others will cooperate so that I can. I confess the selfishness and pride behind this attitude. I confess that I have put myself above others. Above all, I confess that I dishonor You when I insist on my rights, for You alone are Lord. Forgive me of these sins.*

REBUKE

Renounce every lie you have held onto concerning this sense of entitlement. Rebuke the evil spirit(s) that empower you to sin by living in entitlements.

> **Sample Prayer:** *I rebuke and renounce the lies of the enemy right now. I will no longer listen to any word that says I deserve things or have a right to certain things. I bind you, Satan, and every spirit of pride and selfishness that has found access through my sin of entitlement. Be gone, in Jesus' name!*

REPLACE

Affirm that you release all rights to Him as you humble yourself in His presence. Choose to take up your cross against every indication of a sense of entitlement.

> **Sample Prayer:** *Lord, I declare that in Your grace and power I will live a life that reflects that of Jesus Christ, the life of a servant. I will regularly deny myself, and take up my opportunity to sacrifice my entitlements.*

RECEIVE

Open your heart to be filled with the power of His Spirit to lead, guide, and enable you to surrender entitlements. Thank God for His forgiveness of this insidious and ugly sin. Receive His cleansing as He makes you white as snow in His presence.

Sample Prayer: *I ask Your Holy Spirit to now fill me up, so I can humbly submit to You and the others whom You bring into my life. Lord, thank You for forgiving me of this sin of entitlement. Thank You for freely receiving me to Yourself and cleansing me of all unrighteousness.*

WALKING IN THE OPPOSITE SPIRIT

- ❑ These are not easy strongholds to tear down. To walk in the opposite spirit of entitlements is to humble yourself and become a servant. It includes making obedience to God and His Kingdom values priority and to make choices that put other peoples' needs in front of your own.

- ❑ You must continue to identify those things for which you feel entitled and release them to God. Each morning take the time to give Him the right to manage your time, your relationships, your resources, and your decisions.

- ❑ I willingly release my rights to the Lord, for, in truth, everything is from Him, to Him, and through Him.

- ❑ I choose to minister to my family instead of demanding they meet my expectations of them.

- ❑ I will trust that God will meet my needs as He sees fit, and no longer demand it happen in a certain way.

- ❑ As an adult, I release my parents from anything I have felt they owed me—emotionally, financially, or physically.

- ❑ I will yield my time to the Lord and no longer insist that I have a right to do what I want.

- ❑ I will humble myself with other believers and ask them to give me input about my spiritual journey.

- ❑ I will replace selfishness with service and pride with humility before others.

- ❑ I will not insist that I get credit for anything, but will rejoice whenever God chooses to use me for His glory.

- ❑ I will have the same attitude Jesus had when He was willing to give His life and be made of no reputation.

SCRIPTURES:

Luke 9:23
And He was saying to them all, "If anyone wishes to come after Me, he must deny himself, and take up his cross daily and follow Me."

Colossians 3:17, 23–24
Whatever you do, in word or deed, do all in the name of the Lord Jesus, giving thanks through Him to God the Father…Whatever you do, do your work heartily, as for the Lord rather than for men, knowing that from the Lord you will receive the reward of the inheritance. It is the Lord Christ whom you serve.

Mark 8:35
Sitting down, He called the twelve and said to them, "If anyone wants to be first, he shall be last of all and servant of all."

NOTES:

FEAR

According to Webster's dictionary, fear includes the painful emotion or passion excited by an expectation of evil or the apprehension of impending danger.

Fear permeates our culture. It bombards us from the outside in—from the plethora of horror films in the theaters to the sensationalizing of bad news in the media to the exploitation of consumers by advertisers selling just about everything. Fear also assaults us from the inside out –fear of rejection, fear of man, fear of failure, fear of sickness and death—and many others. Terrorism by its very nature is intended to create terror—to create extreme fear!

How many of us have battled fear, the kind of fear that provokes sleepless nights, causes dread, creates panic, and feels paralyzing?

Fear is an anxiety response to a perceived danger, that triggers an emotional reaction. In this sense, fear is typical in the natural realm. And, in a sense, fear is helpful to protect against a threat.

However, there is an ungodly fear that God commands His people to avoid.

Four Principles of Fear

<u>Firstly</u>, whenever there is the possibility of danger, either real or perceived, there will be fear, such as:

- Fear of man
- Fear for provision
- Fear of loss
- Fear of pain or affliction
- Fear of uncertainty of the unknown
- Fear of death

Secondly, fear is typical for a person in the natural context of life.

Thirdly, God commands His people not to live in fear or allow fear to control them.

Fourthly, God commands His people not to *fear* based on His character and Word, for He is greater than all sources of fear.

Ungodly fear can cause:

- Paralysis
- Panic
- Poor decision-making
- Unbelief and distrust toward God

Ungodly fear assesses circumstances or situations outside of God's providence, power, protection, and love.

Biblical Example

The nation of Israel repeatedly modeled ungodly fear, and God regularly judged Israel for their fear and their unbelief. One such time was when the 12 spies came back with a surveillance report of the land God had promised to Israel. Seeing giants in the land, 10 of the 12 were filled with fear and unbelief. The rest of the people were caught up in the spies' fear and, subsequently, their unbelief.

> *Numbers 14:9–12 Do not rebel against the Lord, and don't be afraid of the people of the land. They are only helpless prey to us! They have no protection, but the Lord is with us! Don't be afraid of them!" But the whole community began to talk about stoning Joshua and Caleb. Then the glorious presence of the Lord appeared to all the Israelites at the Tabernacle. And the Lord said to Moses, "How long will these people treat me with contempt? Will they never believe me, even after all the miraculous signs I have done among them? I will disown them and destroy them with a plague.*

In this account, we see:

- Fear debilitates
- Fear dishonors God
- God's people are to be distinct in this world, to live without fear!

Fear's True Issue: When we address the stronghold of fear, it is important to remember that its nature is to *deceive* (mislead by a false appearance or statement; outwit, misrepresent, dupe, misinform, misdirect). The actual source of fear is not necessarily any real loss/danger/sorrow we might anticipate when we operate in that fear. **The real root to fear's power is unbelief towards God, His promises, His character, and His Word.**

Biblical Examples: There are many biblical examples of fear and its judgments. Abraham's fear caused him to lie and put his wife at risk while in Egypt. Israel's fear and unbelief were the reason an entire generation did not see God's land promised to them (Canaan); instead, they died in the wilderness, under judgment. King Saul's fear of Goliath (1 Sam. 17:11) compromised his leadership as Israel's king.

King David demonstrated courage resourced through His faith in God toward the very same Goliath that confronted King Saul. Moses, Joshua, and Caleb were men of faith in the midst of Israel's unbelief concerning the giants and dangers in Canaan.

Fear's Distortion: Behind every fear lurks a lie that creates a distorted view of reality. For example, you may fear that you cannot live without so-and-so or such-and-such. You fear you will be rejected or abandoned. You fear that you or your family will lack provision, or that you or your family will be hurt, or sick or killed. The potential list goes on and on. Your dread of that danger or loss dominates your thoughts and influences your attitudes and actions.

> Fear is one of Satan's primary weapons to disable Gods' people. It must be unmasked, dismantled and destroyed in our individual lives and our corporate life if we are to live powerfully in God.

Fear's Spiritual Essence: Most fears have spiritual energy within them and cause us to be held in their grip, inhibiting our lives and our obedience to God. The New Testament connects fear with the spiritual realms of darkness. Satan's sows his lies into our lives, painting a picture of life without God's goodness and faithfulness. He aims to enslave us with fear so we do not live trusting, surrendered, courageous and dynamic lives of faith. Fear is the expression of our emotions of the unbelief in our hearts and minds.

The Scriptures make it very clear that the Lord wants us to be free of fear. Fear is not merely a state of mind or a bad attitude. It includes a *spirit* (2 Tim. 1:7). Fear is an assignment from the enemy to torment your soul, defile your spirit, and rob you of God's love, power, and a sound mind. Because it is a spiritual force, we must confront it spiritually—not just emotionally or psychologically.

You gain freedom from fear as you:

- allow the power of the Holy Spirit to uncover the presence of fear in your life

- bring your fear to the Cross through forgiveness and affirmation of the truth

- renounce the lies and demonic spirits that give those fears power over our thoughts, emotions, and behaviors

- receive the Holy Spirit's power and take action to move in the opposite spirit: FAITH!

In what areas of your life are you entertaining a spirit of fear? Prayerfully consider the following list and check any of the boxes that apply to you:

DIAGNOSTIC QUESTIONS

Fears Related to God and His Kingdom Life:

There is no fear in love, but perfect love casts out fear because fear involves torment.
1 John 4:18

- ❑ Fear motivates my quiet times and prayer times.
- ❑ I base my relationship with God on my performance; I must earn His attention.
- ❑ I fear failing the Lord or that He will ask too much.
- ❑ I am afraid that giving faithfully to God will challenge my resources.
- ❑ I worry that if I miss God's will, something terrible will happen to me.
- ❑ I live with anxiety over my spiritual life, feeling as if God is just waiting to punish me when I blow it.
- ❑ I am afraid God is going to ask too much of me.
- ❑ I struggle with unnatural thoughts regarding suffering.
- ❑ I tend to fear I might not know God's will or be unable to be faithful to it.
- ❑ I am afraid to step out in faith, fearing that God will not come through.
- ❑ I fear God's manifest power.

I have a fear of . . .

- ❑ The reality of demons
- ❑ Healing
- ❑ Potential persecution
- ❑ Being regarded as off balance or fanatical
- ❑ The cost of following Christ
- ❑ The work of the Holy Spirit
- ❑ False manifestations
- ❑ Spiritual warfare

Fear of Others:

Fear of man will prove to be a snare, but whoever trusts in the Lord is kept safe.
Proverbs 29:25

Hear me, you who know what is right, you people who have my law in your hearts: do not fear the reproach of men or be terrified by their insults. Isaiah 51:7

- ❏ I avoid taking a stand because I worry that I will be wrong or that others won't approve.
- ❏ I feel nervous when I walk into a room full of people.
- ❏ I spend a lot of time wondering what other people think about me.
- ❏ I worry about what others say about me.
- ❏ I become anxious about others' opinions of me.
- ❏ I dread speaking before others.
- ❏ It is hard for me just to be myself around others.
- ❏ I am a big proponent of "going with the flow" and not ruffling other people's feathers, even if I strongly disagree with them.
- ❏ Relating to others on spiritual matters makes me uncomfortable, so I avoid small groups or discipling relationships.
- ❏ If I stand out in a crowd, I will be ridiculed
- ❏ If I initiate relationships, I will be rejected.
- ❏ I withdraw from influential/successful people and those in authority.
- ❏ I often don't do things I think I should or give myself away because I might fail.

Fears of the Future or Bad News:

Surely he will never be shaken; a righteous man will be remembered forever. He will have no fear of bad news; his heart is steadfast, trusting in the Lord. His heart is secure; he will have no fear; in the end, he will look in triumph on his foes. Psalms 112:7–8

- ❏ I am often concerned about things such as finding the right mate or job, or succeeding in the job I have.
- ❏ Many times, I am uneasy about the future without really knowing why.
- ❏ I am generally on edge with worries about my children and try to shield them from bad things all the time.
- ❏ I have one or more obsessive fears (e.g., fear of animals, fear of heights, fear of closed spaces, flying, natural disasters, etc.).
- ❏ I often live like I am waiting for "the other shoe to drop."
- ❏ I often find myself thinking about someone I love being seriously hurt, becoming ill, or dying.
- ❏ I am afraid my marriage will fail or that my children will not "turn out" well.
- ❏ I find it hard to enjoy good times because I wonder how long they will last.
- ❏ I am a "glass half-empty" kind of person.
- ❏ When I make decisions, I often second-guess myself.

- ❑ I fear death.
- ❑ I fear sickness.
- ❑ I fear cancer.
- ❑ I am afraid of my spouse dying.
- ❑ I fear I (or my family) will lack provision.
- ❑ I am afraid of being lonely.
- ❑ I have a phobia(s) of _____, _____.

THE 4 Rs FOR FEAR

REPENTANCE

Aggressively go after the sin of fear by naming all the things about which you are fearful. Confess them as sin and ask God's forgiveness. Repent of the sinful choices you have made because of your fear, especially fear of man instead of God. Agree with God that you have sinned by not believing He will provide, or that He works all things together for your good.

Sample Prayer: *Heavenly Father, I have allowed fear to mark my life and my walk with You. I ask forgiveness for every way that fear has affected my life, and the lives of those I influence. I ask forgiveness for every way I have resisted You and denied Your commands and denied Your character due to fear. I ask forgiveness for fear of man, fear of the future, fear of the unknown, irrational fear, fear of failure, and other fears. These are the result of not trusting You, and I confess them as sin! I now turn in repentance, committing myself to breaking the patterns of fear in my life.*

REBUKE

Renounce every lie you have embraced that keeps you in bondage to fear—fear of failure, fear of the future, fear of others, and an unhealthy fear of God. In the authority of Jesus Christ, resist Satan and any evil spirits that have found a place to oppress you through your sinful fears and close the door firmly on their activity in your life.

Sample Prayer: *In Jesus' name, I renounce every lie and rebuke every evil spirit that has influenced my life because of the sin of fear. I renounce the lie that God cannot be trusted. I renounce the lie that God is not good, and I renounce the lie that God is not sovereign in all things. Through the power of Christ's blood, I am now free from the snare of fear. By the authority of Jesus Christ, I command every spirit of fear to flee.*

REPLACE

Acknowledge and affirm that God holds your life in His hands and will walk with you through every storm. Speak affirmation based on the Scriptures above, and use your personal and relevant declarations to affirm that you now will walk in a spirit of confidence, hope, and faith instead of fear and dread.

RECEIVE

Thank the Lord for how He has freely forgiven you. Request and receive the Holy Spirit's filling, that every place that once was inhabited by the sin of fear will be filled with the fullness of His Spirit.

Sample Prayer: *Father, I receive Your forgiveness. I confidently receive the full measure of Your Spirit, knowing that I am washed by the blood of Christ, who loves me enough to sacrifice Himself. Thank You for filling me entirely now with Your life-giving Holy Spirit, and with the peace, confidence, and trust I need to live free of fear.*

While fear is rooted in deceit and lies, faith is rooted in words of truth that flow out of the true and reliable character of God. Faith is not merely the antidote to fear, but the essential, supernatural dynamic that releases resurrection power and brings heaven on earth. Faith is vastly stronger than fear and enables us not merely to survive this life but to enjoy and release the supernatural and abundant life of God into this world saturated with sin, decay, and death.

WALKING IN THE OPPOSITE SPIRIT

1. **I will recognize God's truth:**
    a. Through the Scriptures themselves
    b. Through God's Word spoken in specific situations (see Acts 27:23–26).

2. **I will receive and believe God's truth,** which means coming into an agreement at a deep heart level and allowing the living Word of God to release faith in me as I receive and meditate on its dynamic truth.

3. **I will declare God's truth over my situation** because when I speak God's Word by faith into a situation, it releases change and power in the spirit realm that will become evident in the natural realm. Our words release God's power.

1 Samuel 17:44–47 "Come here," he said, "and I'll give your flesh to the birds of the air and the beasts of the field!" David said to the Philistine, "You come against me with sword and spear and javelin, but I come against you in the name of the LORD Almighty, the God of the armies of Israel, whom you have defied. This day the LORD will hand you over to me, and I'll strike you down and cut off your head. Today I will give the carcasses of the Philistine army to the birds of the air and the beasts of the earth, and the whole world will know that there is a God in Israel. All those gathered here will know that it is not by sword or spear that the LORD saves; for the battle is the LORD's, and he will give all of you into our hands."

Luke 17:6 He replied, "If you have faith as small as a mustard seed, you can say to this mulberry tree, 'Be uprooted and planted in the sea,' and it will obey you.

4. **I will act on God's truth,**
   Faith must be accompanied by action as led and empowered by the Holy Spirit.

1 Samuel 17:48 As the Philistine moved closer to attack him, David ran quickly toward the battle line to meet him.

SCRIPTURES:

Joshua 1:9
Have I not commanded you? Be strong and courageous! Do not tremble or be dismayed, for the Lord your God is with you wherever you go.

Psalm 118:6
The Lord is for me; I will not fear; what can man do to me?

Proverbs 29:25
The fear of man brings a snare, but he who trusts in the Lord will be exalted.

Isaiah 41:10
Do not fear, for I am with you…Surely I will uphold you with My righteous right hand.

Jeremiah 17:7–8
Blessed is the man who trusts in the Lord and whose trust is in the Lord. For he will be like a tree planted by the water, that extends its roots by a stream and will not fear when the heat comes; but its leaves will be green, and it will not be anxious in a year of drought nor cease to yield fruit.

Philippians 4:6–7
Be anxious for nothing, but in everything by prayer and supplication with thanksgiving let your requests be made known to God. And the peace of God, which surpasses all comprehension, will guard your hearts and your minds in Christ Jesus.

1 Timothy 1:7
For God has not given us a spirit of timidity, but of power, of love, and of discipline.

HOPELESSNESS

Hopelessness is a feeling and belief system that conditions will never improve, that there is no solution to a problem.

For some, hopelessness can lead to depression; for others an extreme outcome would be feeling and thinking that dying would be better than living. Many people who are locked down in hopelessness do not want to live yet they are afraid to die. So they cease to live and merely exist.

For others, their hopelessness is in regard to others. Maybe there are wayward family members who are in a repeating ruinous cycle. Maybe it is others whom they love who have given into hopelessness and passivity.

The world brings hopelessness, because the world's hope is a shell game. The only thing that will bring real hope is reality in truth that comes from God, knowing that He is our Father. Accepting and living in this reality, brings real hope and peace.

Biblical Examples

The Israelites, while in Egyptian bondages as slaves (Exodus 2), lived in hopelessness. They groaned in their slavery and oppressive conditions. They were beaten down. There was no hope for their conditions to change. They took on the posture of victimization and their identity became that of slaves.

We have referenced Gideon (Judges 6–8) at other places in our training. The opening scene of Gideon in Judges 6 is one of dire hopelessness. He succumbed to fear and victimization due to treatment by neighboring tribe of the Midianites and his life experiences.

Who God created Gideon to be was eclipsed by his life experiences and resulting hopelessness. In his thinking, it was futile to change his mindset or circumstances. He believed himself to be inferior and impotent. The angel of the Lord spoke truth to him as to who he truly was, and he had encounters with God that transformed his thinking about himself and his circumstances.

Thoughts on Hopelessness

Often a person who suffers, or has suffered, with bouts of hopelessness, despair, and feeling defeated has experienced much hurt through disappointments, frustrations, abuse, rejection, degradation, and condemnation.

Consequently they struggle to keep their joy, and instead carry bear a heavy load of self-defeating thoughts and feelings. This is a result of unresolved issues and a lot of hurts without healing—hurts that have become a stronghold against them and burdens that are quick to rob them of any hope for positive change.

The Cure for Hopelessness

There is a biblical cure for hopelessness. First, we must redefine reality. Reality is found in God, His truth, and His future. This is realized by removing the myopic lenses to your life and living in light of eternity, recapturing the big picture of life.

Often fear is described *False Evidence Appearing Real*. We need to recapture God's evidence, His truth, His read on a situation and not forget His supernatural power in our lives. God specializes in bringing solution to what appears to be hopeless situations.

A second factor to the cure for hopelessness is releasing others, even loved ones, and situations to God. Often, we carry a burden or responsibility that is not ours to carry. It can happen easily when it involves those we love. We must turn people and situations over to the Lord when we are not primarily responsible for the situation.

Lastly, if we are in a difficult spot, it is real, and we do carry the primary responsibility for the situation; we must trust God. All through the Scriptures you see God bringing supernatural solution to what humanly looks like an impossible condition. Hopelessness does not bring solution, but God and faith in Him does. Get ahold of His truth, His Word, and His character; that is where you put your hope!

One final thought; many times, resolving hopelessness is found in forgiveness. You might need to forgive someone who is responsible for your apparent hopeless situation. All that comes with unforgiveness often contributes to your hopelessness. Truly and fully forgive where necessary.

DIAGNOSTICS OF HOPELESSNESS

Passivity

- ❏ It's hard for me to spend time with God.
- ❏ During the day I find myself thinking, "What good would it do anyway?"
- ❏ I don't initiate conversations with friends, family members, or coworkers.
- ❏ I expect others to approach me and meet me where I am.
- ❏ I don't believe I am needed, so I give up on people or projects.
- ❏ I don't believe it would do any good to confess the sin in my life, so I don't.
- ❏ I have little passion for the things of God (e.g., evangelism, prayer, ministry, God's Word).
- ❏ I "allow" a lot of things to happen in my life.
- ❏ I think the idea of hope is a long shot.
- ❏ I lack motivation to pray or read God's Word.
- ❏ In fact, I lack motivation in most things in my life, or in things having to do with the Lord.
- ❏ I feel that sin will always have control of me, so there's little point in trying to overcome it.

Self-pity and Introspection

- ❏ Most of my thoughts are about me and what I can—and can't—do.
- ❏ A lot of people around me struggle with self-pity.
- ❏ I don't have many close friends.
- ❏ My expectations of others are fairly high.
- ❏ I will never be happy again.
- ❏ I will never get over what happened.
- ❏ I don't see things ever improving.
- ❏ There is no point in trying anymore.
- ❏ What do I have to look forward to?
- ❏ The future is empty for me.
- ❏ It's too late for me, there is nothing I can do to make things better.
- ❏ I have no sense of purpose in life.

Victimization and Inferiority

- ❏ I feel that there's little I can do about my own situation—it seems like I'm at the mercy of other people.
- ❏ I feel that my life is "locked in" because of what others have done to me.
- ❏ I do not like to share my friends with other people because I believe that those who are better than I am or have more than I do will steal them away.
- ❏ I feel protective and tightfisted toward things and relationships because I fear that someone will steal them from me.
- ❏ I don't feel free to share in a group because my comments or ideas would be pounded down or discounted.
- ❏ I am unable to step out with confidence or faith to break new ground.
- ❏ I rarely feel very sure of myself.
- ❏ I "play it safe" in life rather than risk what few resources (or confidence) I have.
- ❏ I resent it when the Lord lifts up others, because I feel that life has not been fair to me.
- ❏ I live a passive life. It's always someone else who makes things happen or leads the charge.

Ingratitude

- ❏ I have a hard time thinking of things for which I can thank the Lord.
- ❏ I can't remember the last time I truly thanked the Lord for all of His provision in my life.
- ❏ I get locked down when I try to pray and thank the Lord.
- ❏ Why should I give thanks when I have little or nothing to hope for?
- ❏ Sometimes I wonder if I will ever get out of this hopeless cycle.

THE 4 Rs FOR HOPELESSNESS

REPENTANCE

Sample Prayer: *Lord Jesus, I ask for Your forgiveness for this sin of carrying hopelessness. I repent of all the ways I have allowed hopelessness to be a part of my life. I see how they have affected me and others around me. I name it as sin. Shame and hopelessness are not from You!* (Go back through the boxes you checked and ask God to forgive you in each area.)

REBUKE

Sample Prayer: *Lord, I renounce the life and ways of hopelessness. That is not who I am and it does not represent You. I rebuke every spirit of hopelessness and despair that has tried to separate me from the love and life of my Heavenly Father. I come against you by the authority of Jesus Christ, and I command you to flee right now. You are liars, and I will no longer listen to you and your deceptions about me. According to the Word of God, I put you under my feet and I crush the influence you have had in my life.*

REPLACE

Sample Prayer: *I replace hopelessness by living a life of joy, peace, courage, boldness, strength, authority, and love that will prompt the world to ask me about the reason for the hope in my life. I will live in the truth of courage, boldness, and confidence that rightfully belongs to those who are children of God.*

RECEIVE

Sample Prayer: *Lord Jesus, I now ask for and receive in faith the infilling of Your Holy Spirit that I might live a supernatural life that lives above all hopelessness. I walk in the hope, confidence, power, and authority that are mine as the child of the King of kings. I am accepted, and a living testimony of God's love, grace, and glory!*

WALKING IN THE OPPOSITE SPIRIT

Part of living free in Christ and walking in true purity and holiness depends on having our minds renewed by God's Word and His Holy Spirit.

- Use the truth of God's Word and the authority you have in Christ to fight and renounce the lies of the enemy when they come back to torment your thoughts.

- Meditate on the promises of God regarding hope.

- Do not allow old mental videos, the words of others, and thoughts of worthlessness or guilt to define you. Those are not who you are!

SCRIPTURES:

Psalm 33:18 (NIV)
But the eyes of the Lord are on those who fear him, on those whose hope is in his unfailing love.

Psalm 119:114
You are my refuge and my shield; your word is my source of hope.

Isaiah 40:31
But those who trust in the LORD will find new strength. They will soar high on wings like eagles. They will run and not grow weary. They will walk and not faint.

Joel 2:26
Once again you will have all the food you want, and you will praise the LORD your God, who does these miracles for you. Never again will my people be disgraced.

Romans 15:13
I pray that God, the source of hope, will fill you completely with joy and peace because you trust in him. Then you will overflow with confident hope through the power of the Holy Spirit.

Romans 8:1
So now there is no condemnation for those who belong to Christ Jesus.

Romans 15:13
May the God of hope fill you with all joy and peace as you trust in him, so that you may overflow with hope by the power of the Holy Spirit.

1 Thessalonians 5:18
Give thanks in all circumstances.

Ephesians 5:20
Giving thanks always and for everything.

Proverbs 23:7
As a man thinks in his heart, so is he.

INSIGNIFICANCE AND INFERIORITY

> Insignificance causes us to believe that we are lower in order, of less value, of less importance, poorer in quality, below average.

Insignificance is the tendency to think we are nothing.

- We cannot believe that who we are and what we do matters!
- We think, *Am I not only one of the billions of people on the earth?*
- Or, *Am I not only an insignificant member of community, family, club, or church?*

Insignificance is a strong inclination to:

- not believe that we can benefit others
- believe that we cannot accomplish something substantial
- feel and believe that we are worthless or unworthy

Biblical Personalities

Insignificance is a common malady. We see it often in the Scriptures; it's not merely a contemporary issue. When God's call came to Moses, he cried out, "Who am I?" and, "I am slow of speech." in Exodus chapters 3 and 4.

Many can relate to Gideon. Israel had been incessantly pummeled and plundered by neighboring nations. For seven years straight, neighboring peoples stole Israel's livestock and crops. The Israelites were beaten down, humiliated, and diminished, filled with fear and inferiority.

Gideon, himself filled with fear and inadequacy, hid in a winepress, in a hole, to thresh grain. Threshing was a job done in high places where the wind could blow away the chaff while the grain kernels fell to the ground. But in Gideon's fear and diminished state, that was too risky for him.

In the midst of Gideon's labor, the angel of the Lord appeared to Gideon and called him *Mighty Hero*. Some translations say, *Valiant Warrior*. Judges 6:11–15 records Gideons's reply:

> *Judges 6:11–15 (NIV) . . . Gideon was threshing wheat in a winepress to keep it from the Midianites. When the angel of the LORD appeared to Gideon, he said, "The LORD is with you, mighty warrior." . . . The LORD turned to him and said, "Go in the strength you have and save Israel out of Midian's hand. Am I not sending you?" "Pardon me, my lord," Gideon replied, "but how can I save Israel? My clan is the weakest in Manasseh, and I am the least in my family."*

Biblically, the meaning of the name Gideon is *he that bruises or breaks, one who destroys*. God's perspective of Gideon and *original design* for him were conflicted. God's perspective…a mighty hero, a valiant warrior. Gideon's perspective…diminished.

Pride and insignificance start from the same place: a focus on us. With insignificance, it often is a focus on my experiences, a focus on injustices I have received, a focus on debilitating words spoken to me by others, a life of love-deficit, or maybe a culture that cultivates insignificance.

Insignificance often finds its roots in a performance-based value for life that evidences itself in position, abilities, status, possessions, successes, or careers.

Insignificance causes us to believe that we are lower in order, of less value and importance to God and others.

The Lord sought out Gideon in this very place, in this hiding place, and radically changed how he viewed himself, his world, and his future. After some encounters with God, Gideon was transformed into a mighty hero, a valiant warrior. He did become one who bruised and destroyed; it was Israel's enemies. He became Israel's deliverer and leader as seen in Judges chapters 6–8.

God seeks out you and me in our places of insignificance to radically change how we see ourselves, and how we live, just as He did Gideon.

Roots of Insignificance

A stronghold of insignificance and inferiority filters our perception of reality with the lie that we are not loved and significant simply for who we are. We and others perceive our value by our position,

abilities, appearance, status, success, possessions, career, or ministry. We fail to recognize that we are unconditionally loved and valued by God.

This stronghold sustains a vicious cycle of hopelessness, striving, and despair: hopelessness that we will never be and do the things we dream of, determination to make it all happen, and feelings of despair and condemnation when we fail.

Recognizing Insignificance

Insignificance is rooted in lies and labels from the enemy, who has opposed you from birth.

- ❏ I am overly conscious of myself and coming up short when comparing myself against others.
- ❏ I often have significant struggles with self-pity, anger, jealousy selfish ambition, and coveting.
- ❏ I feel that I do not belong, and I always get short-changed (self-pity). I can nearly always see how others are greater, or more significant than I am.
- ❏ I believe the Lord does not see me or smile upon me, and I reject the promise that He has a purpose for me.
- ❏ I find no joy in the fact that He has chosen me.
- ❏ I live with buried anger toward people who represent groups in my past who rejected me or made me feel like I was second-class. I am often critical of these types of people because they make me feel inferior.
- ❏ Anger will rise and show itself in diverse ways.

Insignificance's Internal Deceptions

- ❏ I am nobody from nowhere.
- ❏ I am weak and diminished.
- ❏ I have nothing to give to anyone.
- ❏ You don't want to speak to me—why would you?
- ❏ I look down when I walk by people.
- ❏ I don't initiate greeting people; I fear any dimension of rejection.
- ❏ I am shy (or I am often labeled "shy") because I have nothing to say to others.
- ❏ Everyone in my family, including me, is a "nobody."
- ❏ I don't see "strategic significance" to whom and what the Lord created me to be and do.
- ❏ There is much I dislike about myself.
- ❏ I am often self-conscious and internally focused.

Insignificance's Deceptions of Comparison

- ❏ I often compare myself to others.
- ❏ I wonder what others think of me—with insecurity (I live inside other's heads).
- ❏ I constantly compare myself to others, and usually, fall short.
- ❏ I fear to speak to people whom I regard as superior to me.
- ❏ I covet the gifts, abilities, and capacities of others.
- ❏ I am jealous of how other people look, how they act, and how they speak.
- ❏ I limit my friendships with those I regard as my equals or whom I regard as inferior to me.

Insignificance's Deceptions of Diminishment

- ❏ I am fearful or anxious about being responsible for tasks because of inadequacies.
- ❏ I prefer to remain hidden and anonymous and be passed over for assignments.
- ❏ I only want easy tasks I can accomplish with my abilities.
- ❏ I only speak to people with whom I am familiar.
- ❏ I avoid risks in front of individuals (e.g., praying out loud, speaking in front of others, etc.).
- ❏ I prefer being alone because it's safer, easier, and less work.
- ❏ I do not find joy in the Lord's challenges.

Insignificance's Spiritual Deception

- ❏ The Lord does not take my prayers seriously.
- ❏ It's hard for me to believe that God has chosen me for a significant purpose.
- ❏ I feel I am insignificant to the Lord.
- ❏ When people tell me I am "strategic in God's Kingdom," I think they could not possibly be talking to me.
- ❏ The Lord doesn't speak to me.
- ❏ I often question God's presence in my life.
- ❏ I do not believe I have significant spiritual authority.
- ❏ I can't see my destiny (even when someone tries to tell me), or how I will be used to advance the Kingdom—why me?

Insignificance's Self-pity

- ❏ I blame others for not seeing anything good in me; "it's not my fault."
- ❏ My parents weren't very encouraging to me, so that is why I don't believe in myself.
- ❏ "These are just my character traits—God made me this way!"
- ❏ I am a victim of a hard life.
- ❏ No one ever blesses me so don't expect much of me.
- ❏ I feel rejected if I am not encouraged or recognized.

Insignificance's Diminishment of Others

- ❏ I am critical of others because I couldn't or wouldn't do things "that way."
- ❏ I am critical of others when they challenge me because "I can't change."
- ❏ I am critical of others because *I believe that they think* they are superior to me.
- ❏ I withhold blessing from others because I have nothing to give.
- ❏ I withhold blessing from others because my thoughts and encouragement about others don't matter to them.
- ❏ I withhold blessing from others because I do not want them to pass me up (I am threatened and insecure).

Insignificance's Deception to Ambition

- ❏ I do what I think others would like me to do.
- ❏ I say things I believe will cause others to approve of me.
- ❏ I feel insecure if others think poorly of me.
- ❏ I find it hard to cope with failure.
- ❏ Success is a very high priority for me.
- ❏ I judge myself and others by the measure of their success.
- ❏ I see success as something to be attained.
- ❏ I want people to think highly of me.
- ❏ I value my reputation.

THE 4 Rs FOR INSIGNIFICANCE

REPENTANCE

Take responsibility for insignificance.

> **Sample Prayer:** *Lord, I declare my repentance of insignificance. I confess right now that I have allowed it to become a part of my life. I call it out before You as sin. I confess submitting to insignificance in my own life. I break off significance in every area of my life right now by turning in the opposite direction and living in Your truth that I am significant in Jesus Christ and that You regard me as significant.*

REBUKE

Renounce every lie you have held onto concerning your mindset and sin of insignificance in your life. In the authority of Jesus Christ, resist Satan and any evil spirits that have found a place to oppress you through insignificance and insecurity.

> **Sample Prayer:** *I resist and bind the lies of the enemy right now. Their attack on my life around insignificance is broken. I refuse to believe that I am insignificant. I rebuke every evil spirit that energizes insignificance in my life. I command you to the feet of Jesus to receive your judgment from Him.*

REPLACE

It takes an absolute hatred for the sin of insignificance in order to walk free of it. It is a deep cleansing of part of your personality, including your ways of thinking, your reactions, and your motives. When you begin to feel internal angst, stop and ask the Lord if insignificance is the issue. If it is, confess it and receive His cleansing. Acknowledge and affirm that God is the only One worthy of controlling your life and that His plans for you are perfect in every way.

RECEIVE

Thank the Lord that He has totally forgiven you. Receive His full cleansing and rejoice. Request the filling of the Holy Spirit to fill every place that was once inhabited by the sin of insignificance.

Sample Prayer: *Lord, I receive Your forgiveness for the sin of control in my life. I receive Your love for me. Fill me with Your Holy Spirit that I may live supernaturally in the freedom of faith and trust in You and to serve others.*

WALKING IN THE OPPOSITE SPIRIT

The secret is to take our eyes off of ourselves and turn to the Lord, allowing Him to define us, to clothe us in righteousness, to seat us with Him in heaven, and to bestow gifts upon us. We choose to believe what God says about us, and not what we or others (or even circumstances) might indicate about us.

SCRIPTURES:

God infinitely loves me as His child. (Ephesians 3:16–20)

I am God's workmanship. (Ephesians. 2:10)

God highly favors me.

I am confident of God's unconditional love for me. (1 John 3:1)

I have a spirit of power, love, and a sound mind. (2 Timothy 1:7)

God chooses me for His purposes. (Ephesians 2:10)

I have been given authority in Jesus Christ. (Luke 10:19)

I am the salt of the earth and the light of the world. (Matthew 5:13–14)

I am secure in God's love and highly favored. (Romans 8:38)

I am complete in Christ. (Colossians 1:10)

I can freely enter God's presence. (Hebrews 4:14–16)

God's Kingdom is within me. (Luke 17:20–21)

God directs my path when I seek Him. (Proverbs 3:5–6)

I am free from condemnation. (Romans 8:1–2)

NOTES: _____
_____
_____
_____

JEALOUSY AND SELFISH AMBITION

To be jealous is to be envious of another's success, achievements, advantages, positions, possessions, etc.

When you follow the desires of your sinful nature, your lives will produce evil results. The results can include sexual immorality, impure thoughts, eagerness for lustful pleasure, idolatry, participation in demonic activities, hostility, quarreling, jealousy, outbursts of anger, selfish ambition, divisions, the feeling that everyone is wrong except those in your own little group, envy, drunkenness, wild parties, and other kinds of sin. (Galatians 5:19–21)

Selfish ambition is to inordinately or wrongly desire wealth, possessions, status, or stature for one's own benefit and promotion.

But if you have bitter jealousy and selfish ambition in your heart, do not be arrogant and so lie against the truth. This wisdom is not that which comes down from above, but is earthly, natural, demonic. For where jealousy and selfish ambition exist, there is disorder and every evil thing. (James 3:14–16)

Jealousy and covetousness keep us from truly loving God, others, and ourselves. They also keep us from being content in everything the Father has given us. They take away our joy and put us in a place of self-focus, self-pity, discontentment, hopelessness, ingratitude, grumbling, and anxiety. Jealousy and selfish ambition inhibit our ability to form close relationships. They rob us of our joy and create hostility, bitterness, and resentment.

Intimately connected to jealousy and selfish ambition is covetousness. Covetousness wrongly desires something you do not have and often what others do have. To obtain something through jealousy, selfish ambition, and covetousness most often costs others through injustices and betrayals. In the long run, it also will cost the person who lives with jealousy and selfish ambition.

We again see this sin and stronghold in the life and actions of Lucifer toward God. The same sin found is demonstrated in so many lives in the Scriptures. The apostles desired places of position. In fact, in one instance so did the mother of a couple of disciples. We read in Matthew 20 that the mother of James and John, two of Jesus' disciples, came to request that her sons sit on thrones with Jesus in His Kingdom, one on the left and another on the right.

When the other disciples heard James's and John's request, they became infuriated. Their response was quick and animated. Jealousy and selfish ambition quickly surfaced. Jesus taught them that humility and servanthood are the Kingdom mandates. In fact, in one instance, Jesus brought a child before His disciples as an object lesson on this subject.

Another of Jesus' disciples, being filled with selfish ambition, could not accept Jesus' Kingdom mission. Due to his selfish ambition, he betrayed Jesus and offered him up to the religious leaders to for crucifixion. His name was Judas.

James 3 states that where jealousy and selfish ambition exist, there is disorder and every evil thing. That was indeed the case with Lucifer and his rebellion against God. Likewise, it was true regarding Judas. And it is still true today.

Jealousy and selfish ambition are dangerous and must be dealt with ruthlessly in our lives.

The core of jealousy and selfish ambition (check all boxes that apply to your life):

1. It says, "<u>I want</u> something that you have."

    - ❏ I have buried or outward anger that is actually anger toward God over what I do not possess.
    - ❏ Preoccupation with the accumulation of "things." There is a sense of entitlement that "I deserve to live a certain way," or, "I deserve to present myself in a certain way," or, "I deserve certain things."
    - ❏ My life is marked by discontentment, because of a preoccupation with a coveted position, role, or gift.

2. <u>Unresolved hurts</u> in my life can develop into jealousy or disdain toward others.

    - ❏ I rise up around others who appear to have a loving and fulfilling marriage and friendship, or perceivably satisfying relationships.
    - ❏ I carry anger and resentment toward those close to me whom I perceive as withholding.
    - ❏ I diminish or push away those toward whom I have expressed jealousy.

3. <u>Ingratitude</u> and areas of entitlements.

    - ❏ I feel that I am getting a "raw deal." I should have what others have.

- ❏ I get angry over being inconvenienced.
- ❏ I possess a timeline of opportunities that I feel I merit.
- ❏ I have a hard time thanking God for what He has done in my life. Thanksgiving plays a small role in my life.

4. **Pride** is at the core of jealousy/selfish ambition.
   - ❏ I believe I deserve what another person has.
   - ❏ I tend to prove that I am better than others around me.
   - ❏ I mentally build a case why I am better than others.
   - ❏ I don't believe what the Lord says about me, so I covet another's gifting.
   - ❏ In my actions I make others feel less so I elevate myself.
   - ❏ I tear others down with my words because I am jealous of their gifting.
   - ❏ I spend a lot of time thinking about myself and what I deserve.

5. **Unbelief** is at the core of jealousy/selfish ambition.
   - ❏ I don't believe what God's written Word says about me.
   - ❏ My identity and value lie in what I do or can accomplish.
   - ❏ I want what others have because I don't believe the Lord has my highest good in mind.
   - ❏ I need to accomplish things for myself because the Lord won't come through for me.
   - ❏ I compare the way I appear to the way others look.
   - ❏ I want other's material possessions; because I don't believe the Lord will take care of me.
   - ❏ I have a hard time believing that the Lord loves me, wants the best for me, and will provide for my every need.
   - ❏ I pray for myself most often and have a hard time praying/thinking about others.

6. **Inferiority** is at the core of jealousy/selfish ambition.
   - ❏ I am jealous of what other people look like and how they act.
   - ❏ I compare myself to others, usually falling short.
   - ❏ I find myself saying, "I'll never be like _____."
   - ❏ I get angry or feel deflated when I don't receive what I want.
   - ❏ I have a hard time when other people are blessed.
   - ❏ When I am truthful with myself, I don't like it when the Lord elevates one of my peers.

- ❏ I am out to prove how worthy I am.
- ❏ My feelings of insignificance/inferiority are elevated by what someone else has (their possessions, for example).

Specific forms of jealousy and selfish ambition that need to be destroyed:

- ❏ Regarding appearance
- ❏ Regarding spiritual gifting and skills
- ❏ Regarding material possessions
- ❏ Concerning position and responsibilities
- ❏ Concerning relationships
- ❏ Regarding friendships; wanting to be another's most significant friend
- ❏ Regarding the Lord's blessing in another person's life
- ❏ Toward a friend
- ❏ Toward a sibling or relative
- ❏ Regarding realms of responsibility
- ❏ Concerning realms of influence

THE 4 Rs FOR JEALOUSY

REPENTANCE

Sample Prayer: *Lord, I ask for You to forgive me for the sin of jealousy, selfish ambition, and covetousness. I call these things sin, Lord, and I hate them. I repent of jealousy, selfish ambition, and covetousness right now. I turn from them. (Specifically ask forgiveness for each box you checked, as well as any sins that come to mind associated with each category.) I ask forgiveness for _____. I see it and call it sin. I now turn to repentance, committing myself to breaking the patterns of jealousy and covetousness in my life.*

REBUKE

Sample Prayer: *I rebuke every spirit that has empowered jealousy, selfish ambition, and covetousness in my life. I command you to flee in the name of Jesus Christ. I reject your lies and how you have schemed against me for so long. I will not listen to these lies any longer. You are defeated and have no legal hold on me.*

REPLACE

Sample Prayer: *I stand in agreement with the Word of God. I agree with who God is and what He says about me. I will live content in God's will and purposes in my life and find great delight in who God created me to be and look to serve Him and others.*

RECEIVE

Sample Prayer: *Holy Spirit, fill me to live in godly obedience and character in supernatural capacities. Lord Jesus, I receive Your forgiveness. Your Word says that when I confess my sins, You are faithful and just to forgive my sins and cleanse me from all unrighteousness. Thank You, Lord, for Your forgiving power and love for me.*

WALKING IN THE OPPOSITE SPIRIT

- ❑ When tempted with jealousy, selfish ambition, or coveting thoughts, I will move in the opposite spirit by praying a blessing on the person toward whom those thoughts were directed. Pray that the Lord would pour His blessings and His anointing on them. Pray that the Lord would expand his or her territory.
- ❑ I can celebrate other's successes with them.
- ❑ Push others into their calling with encouraging words and actions.
- ❑ The successes of others add to my joy.
- ❑ I rejoice in God's creation and His unique design of other individuals.
- ❑ Instead of holding a jealous thought toward another, I will choose to encourage him/her with affirming words.

SCRIPTURES:

I am assured that all things work together for good.
Romans 8:28
And we know that God causes everything to work together for the good of those who love God and are called according to his purpose for them.

I have been chosen and appointed by God to bear fruit.
John 15:16
You didn't choose me. I chose you. I appointed you to go and produce fruit that will last, so that the Father will give you whatever you ask for, using my name.

I am a temple of God.
1 Corinthians 3:16
Don't you realize that all of you together are the temple of God and that the Spirit of God lives in you?

We are blessed with every spiritual blessing in Christ.
Ephesians 1:3
How we praise God, the Father of our Lord Jesus Christ, who has blessed us with every spiritual blessing in the heavenly realms because we belong to Christ.

We are God's Masterpiece.
Ephesians 2:10
For we are God's masterpiece. He has created us anew in Christ Jesus, so that we can do the good things he planned for us long ago.

I am satisfied – I am fulfilled – I am full of joy and I am free.
Galatians 5:1
So Christ has really set us free. Now make sure that you stay free, and don't get tied up again in slavery to the law.

NOTES:

Passivity is pattern of inactivity, allowing yourself to be acted upon, holding back, laying low, a hesitancy to take the initiative or action mainly related to biblical obedience, yielding without resistance.

Passivity may seem like an innocent personality trait. Most of us would wonder how it could be considered sin.

Passivity may be insidiously sinful, but it is destructive, it devastates, it opens up a broad base of operation for Satan and his schemes to be successful.

Jesus' Teaching: Jesus taught that force must take the Kingdom of God. "The kingdom of heaven has been forcefully advancing," He said, "and forceful men lay hold of it" (Matthew 11:12, NIV). Jesus wasn't talking about building God's Kingdom through physical violence. He was talking about effort, initiative, and action.

The words "force" and "forceful" that Jesus used in this text of Scripture are the Greek words *biastes* and *biazo*, which means "to press violently or force one's way into." The same word is used to refer to the "pounding of the surf" in Acts 27:41. The analogy is that as powerful waves beat relentlessly and unceasingly on the ocean shore, so our lives are to be persevering in our pursuit of and obedience to God.

Biblical Example:

Eli was a priest for Israel at the end of the period of the judges. The last verse in the book of judges says, "In those days Israel had no king; all the people did what was right in their own eyes." There was no respect for God or His ways even among the religious leaders; of which Eli is an example.

1 Samuel 2:12–22 Now the sons of Eli were scoundrels who had no respect for the LORD or their duties as priests. . . . So the sin of these young men was very serious in the LORD's sight, for they treated the LORD's offerings with contempt. . . . Now Eli was very old, but he was aware of what his sons were doing to the people of Israel. He knew, for instance, that his sons were seducing the young women who assisted at the entrance of the Tabernacle.

Eli was hearing reports from the people concerning the ungodliness of his sons who were priests and under his government as Israel's chief priest. Eli was not ignorant of the vile lives and lifestyle of his sons, who were spiritual leaders in Israel. Then a man of God came to him with a message from the Lord. We read this message in 1 Samuel 2:30–34.

"Therefore, the LORD, the God of Israel, says: I promised that your branch of the tribe of Levi would always be my priests. But I will honor those who honor me, and I will despise those who think lightly of me. The time is coming when I will put an end to your family, so it will no longer serve as my priests. All the members of your family will die before their time. None will reach old age. You will watch with envy as I pour out prosperity on the people of Israel. But no members of your family will ever live out their days. The few not cut off from serving at my altar will survive, but only so their eyes can go blind and their hearts break, and their children will die a violent death. And to prove that what I have said will come true, I will cause your two sons, Hophni and Phinehas, to die on the same day!"

God again reiterated this through a young man, a teenage boy named Samuel. God warned Eli multiple times. But Eli was passive!

Soon after that, Israel found itself at war with—and defeated by—the Philistines. The Philistines captured the Ark of the Covenant, and Eli's two sons died on the same day. Word got back to Eli. 1 Samuel 4:18 describes what followed.

"When the messenger mentioned what had happened to the Ark of God, Eli fell backward from his seat beside the gate. He broke his neck and died, for he was old and overweight.

This account is a description and paints a picture of passivity and its consequences. Jesus offered a contrast to the stronghold of passivity in the Kingdom parable found in Matthew 13:44–46."

"The kingdom of heaven is like treasure hidden in a field. When a man found it, he hid it again, and then in his joy went and sold all he had and bought that field. "Again, the kingdom of heaven is like a merchant looking for fine pearls. When he found one of great value, he went away and sold everything he had and bought it."

Characteristics of Passivity:

The opposite of passivity is not activism but taking the initiative in obedience to the Lord's commands, directives, and Kingdom values. Passivity is firmly connected to fear of failure, fear of rejection, unbelief, insignificance, inadequacy, and insecurities.

Passivity also has hallmarks of procrastination, deflection of responsibility, casting blame, independence, co-dependency, comparison for personal validation, victimization, apathy, and lethargy.

It often is connected to anger, both passive-aggressive and overt. Many times there is a relationship to passivity and hesitation to expose yourself to risk or responsibility due to fear of failure or harm. Another characteristic of passivity is that while a person demonstrates passivity in specific areas of life, in other areas that same person initiates and exerts himself or herself.

We cannot lose sight of the fact that passivity fundamentally is rebellion. It is doing what you want when you want by not doing what God has directed.

Exhortation toward Passivity:

To indeed live free of the enemy's assaults on our lives, and for God's Kingdom to advance in our lives and our world, we must move in the force, power, and authority of Jesus Christ. We are empowered to be "more than conquerors" in Him (Romans 8:37).

The spirit of passivity, however, seeks to crush the force of Christ's power and authority in you. It endeavors to render you weak, impotent, and useless. It attacks you at the core of God's original design for you—which is to be the bearer of His image and authority on earth.

Passivity is inactivity where godly obedience should be taking place. As mentioned, it can include allowing oneself to be unhelpfully acted upon, submitting without objection or resistance, hesitation on areas of biblical obedience, and lack of initiation. It compromises relationships (especially and most destructively in marriages and parenting), ministries, careers, and many other strategic areas of life by merely preventing people from doing what they were created and called to do.

Prayerfully consider the following indicators of passivity. Check any boxes that may apply to you:

PASSIVITY DIAGNOSTICS:

Lacking Initiation:

- ❏ I fail to initiate conversations with others and wait instead for someone to initiate conversation with me.
- ❏ I hesitate initiating relationships . . .
    - ❏ I am slow to contact others or return others' communication initiatives toward me.
    - ❏ I don't initiate activities with others.
    - ❏ I hold back for others to first approach me.

- ❏ I have no urgency or hunger in my spiritual relationship with the Lord.
- ❏ I am not motivated to read Scripture, pray, serve, or worship the Lord.
- ❏ I know I need to press into knowing God more intimately, but I feel no urgency about spending time with Him.
- ❏ I need to receive revelation from God, healing, a release of God's power in my life, etc. and I am waiting for God to do it.
- ❏ I tend to be satisfied with the status quo in my walk with God.
- ❏ I hesitate to make clear decisions for fear of getting it wrong or being confronted with the unforeseen.
- ❏ I regularly fail to do or complete jobs that need to be done.
- ❏ I fear moving out of my comfort zone.

Independent Individualism:

- ❏ I feel like I don't need anyone else.
- ❏ I do not offer help or serve to others.
- ❏ I resist interdependence.
- ❏ I tend to observe the activities of others; I rarely feel motivated or worthy to join in.
- ❏ I don't like to do what everyone else does; I am my own person.
- ❏ I see myself as more of a "private" Christian; I am reserved and keep to myself.
- ❏ I often find myself watching the interactions of others, but not engaging myself.
- ❏ The Church has so many flaws; I will serve God on my own and in my own way.

Passivity as Disobedience/Rebellion:

- ❏ I resist obedience to the Lord by allowing sins to remain in my life:
    - ❏ I do not seek the place of repentance;
    - ❏ I have become familiar with and indifferent toward sins in my life;
    - ❏ I do not believe it would do any good to take authority over sins in my life.
- ❏ I resist God's forgiveness by not taking the authority Jesus has given me over my sin.
- ❏ (Husband/Father) I do not lead my family strongly. I defer much of the leadership of our family to my wife.

- ☐ I am more inclined to do what I want to do than what I ought to do.
- ☐ I know there are sinful patterns/strongholds I need to deal with in my life, but I am not very motivated to go after them.
- ☐ When God shows me something or speaks into my life, I put off taking any direct action.
- ☐ I am timid about leading out, even when God puts me in that position.
- ☐ I often look back and wonder why I haven't done the things I intended to do, especially in spiritual matters.

Self-pity:

- ☐ I have always struggled with depression, insecurity, shyness, fear, loneliness, etc.; I doubt any change could be a reality.
    - ☐ Spiritually: I'm all right with my walk with God right now.
    - ☐ Emotionally: I have always struggled, so why should I worry about it and try to change?
    - ☐ Physically: I don't care what others think of my appearance. Too bad if they don't like what they see; I don't need them anyway.
- ☐ I am comfortable with the way I am.
- ☐ I am a victim; I don't know how not to be a victim.
- ☐ Others are wrong to push me to become someone I am not.
- ☐ I blame others for the way that I am.

Passivity's Lies:

- ☐ Passivity is part of my personality.
- ☐ If I am meant to step out and initiate, I would really "feel like it."
- ☐ I will be a failure if I try to initiate.
- ☐ At least there is *some* comfort in self-pity and being a victim.
- ☐ I don't need anyone telling me how to act!

THE 4 Rs FOR PASSIVITY

REPENTANCE

Take responsibility for passivity by naming every area where you have been hesitant or resistant to do the things you need to do. Confess the sins of procrastination, which is nothing more than disobedience.

> **Sample Prayer:** *Father, I ask for Your forgiveness for this sin of living in passivity and for the patterns of passivity in my life. I see how it has affected me and those around me. I call it sin. Passivity is not from You! (Go back and confess each specific box that you checked.) I repent of every way that passivity has been a part of my personality and lifestyle and I commit to breaking the patterns of it in my life.*

REBUKE

Renounce every lie you have embraced that has enabled you to continue this sin of passivity. Resist the efforts and work of Satan's kingdom, which doesn't really care how good your intentions are, as long as you do not follow through. Exercise your authority over the related demonic beings.

> **Sample Prayer:** *I rebuke every unclean spirit attacking me with lies that have caused me to be passive in many areas of my life! I come against you by the authority of Jesus Christ—and I command you to flee right now! I resist every work of the evil one to keep me in passivity and sever the power of all demonic oppression against my identity and call as a strong, active warrior for Jesus Christ.*

REPLACE

Speak the truth of God's Word over every area of passivity in your life, committing by the power of God's Spirit to walk in bold faith and action in the future. Use God's truth listed in Scripture or others to replace patterns of passivity and your old tendency to hide behind it.

> **Sample Prayer:** *I declare by God's grace that I will live life so as to obey God immediately, completely, and joyfully in every area of my life as directed by His Word. In God's power, I will initiate in areas of ministry and relational responsibility. I will live in active dependence with God and interdependence with others. I will pursue God and His fullness of life for me with all my heart, mind, and strength.*

RECEIVE

Thank the Lord that He has forgiven you from the sin of passivity. Rejoice and receive the fullness of His Spirit, who will energize you to fulfill every step of obedience.

Sample Prayer: *Holy Spirit, fill me—be released in me to my life for Jesus with a supernatural force of obedience and passion. I joyfully receive Your work in my life.*

WALKING IN THE OPPOSITE SPIRIT

- ❑ Father, You are a God of strength and action, and You saved me to fulfill Your purpose.
- ❑ I choose now to give my life to You, to listen to Your voice, and to embrace my position in You.
- ❑ I replace fear of moving out of my comfort zone with determination to act in obedience to Your call.
- ❑ I will initiate conversations with others. I will go to them and not wait for them to come to me.
- ❑ I will resist self-centeredness and reach out in ministry to others by Your grace.
- ❑ I will stop procrastinating and instead take action promptly. I will resist the lie of always waiting for a "better time."
- ❑ Even when I "don't feel like it," I will take authority over sin patterns such as self-pity and victimization.
- ❑ I will no longer live in the lie that it doesn't matter what I do, and instead, will pursue Your pleasure in even small steps of obedience.
- ❑ I will go out of my way to bless people.
- ❑ I will replace the excuse of thinking I will never change with the truth that Your Spirit is at work within me to make me like Jesus.
- ❑ I will cry out in hunger to grow spiritually.
- ❑ (Husbands) I will lead my family according to Your direction, and will not shrink back in intimidation, insecurity, fear, or laziness.
- ❑ I will use the authority You have granted me to wage war against the evil one in my life and family.

SCRIPTURES:

Proverbs 6:9
How long will you lie down, O sluggard? When will you arise from your sleep? "A little sleep, a little slumber, a little folding of the hands to rest." Your poverty will come in like a vagabond and your need like an armed man.

Daniel 11:32
The people who know their God will display strength and take action.

John 15:16a
You did not choose Me but I chose you, and appointed you that you would go and bear fruit, and that your fruit would remain.

Philippians 4:13
I can do all things through Him who strengthens me.

2 Timothy 1:7
For God has not given us a spirit of timidity, but of power, love, and discipline.

Hebrews 6:11–12
And we desire that each one of you show the same diligence so as to realize the full assurance of hope until the end, so that you will not be sluggish, but imitators of those who through faith and patience inherit the promises.

NOTES:

Pride (and arrogance) is defined as "an overly high opinion of oneself; self-absorbed; exaggerated self-esteem; conceit; giving oneself an undue degree of importance; haughty."

When pride comes, then comes disgrace, but with humility comes wisdom.
Proverbs 11:2

The first expression of *pride* that leads to sin is found in Lucifer who, being filled with pride, became evil, and desired to take on a position and role that were not his; they belonged to God. It is believed the following Scriptures depict this event.

Isaiah 14:12–14 (ESV) *How you are fallen from heaven, O Day Star, son of Dawn! How you are cut down to the ground, you who laid the nations low! You said in your heart, 'I will ascend to heaven; above the stars of God I will set my throne on high; I will sit on the mount of assembly in the far reaches of the north; I will ascend above the heights of the clouds; I will make myself like the Most High.'*

Ezekiel 28:14–15, 17 (ESV) *You were an anointed guardian cherub. I placed you; you were on the holy mountain of God; in the midst of the stones of fire you walked. You were blameless in your ways from the day you were created, till unrighteousness was found in you. Your heart was proud because of your beauty; you corrupted your wisdom for the sake of your splendor. I cast you to the ground; I exposed you before kings, to feast their eyes on you.*

The Scriptures provide many examples of people who were filled with pride, and subsequently suffered demise because of it. James 4:6 clearly states that God resists the proud but gives His favor to the humble.

"Resist" means *"withstand; oppose; fend off; stand firm against, withstand the action of, oppose actively; work against."* Imagine God *resisting* you. The Scriptures state that is what happens to those who live in a spirit of pride and arrogance.

King Uzziah's Battle with Pride

We read in 2 Chronicles 26 about the life of Uzziah, who became king of Judah at the age of 16 and ruled for 52 years. He sat under the spiritual mentoring of the prophet Jeremiah and followed Jeremiah's counsel. King Uzziah led Judah to many great conquests, strengthened the walls of Jerusalem, built cisterns, and caused the land to prosper. *"As long as he sought the Lord, God gave him success."* (2 Chronicles 26:3)

The connection seems very clear. Uzziah relied on the Lord for direction, help and strength. He humbled himself—king or no king. God is not impressed with titles that we bestow on each other. God was then—and still is—more concerned about our heart, our ability to understand that we can do NOTHING without Him. Our foolish plans, our weak strength, and our inability to see the future continually point to our need to depend on the Lord.

As Uzziah's story continues, his army became "a mean, lean, fighting' machine" with all the latest technology; the surrounding armies feared them. *"His fame spread far and wide, for he was greatly helped until he became powerful."* (2 Chron. 26:15)

Check out the turning point for Uzziah: *"But after Uzziah became powerful, his PRIDE led to his downfall, and he was unfaithful to the Lord his God."* (2 Chron. 26:16). In his pride, Uzziah placed himself above God's established authorities (the priests). He went into the temple and presented his own offerings before God—something only the priests were allowed to do. Pride convinced him that he was above everyone else and answered to no one; he was the king, after all, and could do whatever he desired.

Notice God's strong response to Uzziah's pride and arrogance. Eighty courageous priests confronted him in the temple as he offered incense to the Lord. His reaction? *"He flew into a rage and while raging the Lord struck him with leprosy."* (2 Chron. 26:19). The chapter closes with Uzziah clinging to pride right up to the sad and difficult end of his life. *"King Uzziah had leprosy until the day he died. He lived in a separate house, leprous and excluded from the temple of the Lord. Jotham, his son, had charge of the palace and governed the people of the land."* (2 Chron. 26:21)

What did Uzziah's pride and arrogance gain for him? It brought God's resistance. It brought God's judgment, separation from the house of God, separation from those he loved, and greatly reduced the scope and length of his reign as king. In a sense, Uzziah became a prisoner of his own pride and arrogance.

Pride is destructive. Pride was the beginning of Lucifer's downfall. The Scriptures speak a lot about pride and the perils associated with pride. This includes the warning of placing people in positions of leadership and authority prematurely, lest they succumb to the same fate as Lucifer.

Evidence of living out of pride and arrogance:

- living only for your own benefit
- regarding ourselves as more important than others
- thinking and acting selfishly
- creating strife, division and chaos
- gossiping and tearing down others
- regarding others with jealousy
- taking offense easily and quickly
- becoming angry when our "rights" are violated
- viewing ourselves above others; we will not "lower" ourselves to serve others
- living with entitlements
- displaying a "my way or the highway" attitude
- finding it difficult to bend or to be flexible.

Characteristics of pride and arrogance:

- A lean towards defensiveness. Shown on a continuum, it would move beyond defensiveness to combativeness
- The forceful control and manipulation of other people (shutting others down verbally)
- The desire to compete in arenas that have winners and losers
- Not drawn to "nameless and faceless" assignments.
- Want some of the recognition or "glory" for the assignment
- Posturing or positioning myself so that my gifts, possessions, strengths, and abilities are accentuated and recognized

- Everyone else's sins are worse than mine (Leads to denial of the gravity of my own sins.)
- Distaste for taking instructions
- Inward desire to see other people fail; enjoy the failures of others
- Refusal to function in certain tasks that are "beneath" me

RECOGNIZING PRIDE

(Check the boxes that apply to you)

- ❑ I find it easy to see the shortcomings and sins of others, but often I cannot see my own.
- ❑ I am critical of the positions, blessings, and gifts of others.
- ❑ I want others to recognize me and my abilities, and I drop frequent hints—some subtle, some not so subtle—in praise of myself.
- ❑ I am willing to gossip and tear down others, so I will look better than them,
- ❑ I am unwilling to "give in" for the sake of others.
- ❑ I find it easy to follow my own advice, my own direction, and my own wisdom.
- ❑ I find it hard to receive and accept "godly advice, wisdom and correction" from others.
- ❑ I see myself as my own "leader and authority."
- ❑ I am self-sufficient; I do not need others—and sometimes I don't need God.
- ❑ I tend to get involved in arguments and conflicts.
- ❑ I consider myself "independent" and "self-made"
- ❑ I often refer to my own "Christian" activities, "religious background," or "spiritual life" as a benchmark for others.

THE OPPOSITE SPIRIT—"HUMILITY"

Now look at what God does for the humble of heart and mind. Webster defines **favor** as "approve, support, endorse; regard or treat with special advantages, special privileges, preferred treatment." Wow!! Who doesn't want to receive *that* from the Lord?

Humility is;

- a willingness to be known for who we really are
- a total dependence on God's sufficiency
- a complete submission to the Lordship of Christ
- an absolute obedience to the Word and truth of God

THE 4 Rs FOR PRIDE

REPENTANCE

Sample Prayer: *Jesus, I ask forgiveness for the sin of pride/arrogance. I ask forgiveness for every way it has affected my relationship with You and others. (Specifically ask forgiveness for each box you checked as well as any sins that come to mind associated with each category.) I ask forgiveness for _____(list the ways pride has played out in your life)_____. I see it and call it sin. I now turn in repentance and commit myself to breaking the patterns of pride in my life.*

REBUKE

Sample Prayer: *In Jesus' name and authority, I rebuke every evil spirit that empowered pride/arrogance in my life and command you to the feet of Jesus. In Jesus' name, I rebuke every spirit that was given a foothold in my life due to pride. In the name of Jesus, every deceiving and lying spirit must go to the feet of Jesus to receive His judgment.*

REPLACE

Sample Prayer: *I replace the sin of pride/arrogance by walking in humility. I will specifically live out humility by _____ (list specific actions and attitudes of humility) _____.*

RECEIVE

Sample Prayer: *Lord, fill me with Your Holy Spirit that I may live supernaturally in the humility of Jesus Christ before You and toward others. I receive Your forgiveness for the sin of pride in my life. I receive Your love for me.*

WALKING IN THE OPPOSITE SPIRIT

- ❏ I will view myself as a servant to everyone.
- ❏ I will grow in the character of Christ.
- ❏ I will look for the opportunity to see others "lifted up."

- ❑ I will see myself in accord with the ways God sees me.
- ❑ I will acknowledge my shortcomings and sins in the presence of others, so I can be encouraged in my walk with the Lord.
- ❑ I will acknowledge that all that I am, all that I have, and all that I do come to me from the Lord, and I can take no claim for myself.
- ❑ I will pray consistently for God to reveal to me any pride or arrogance that may be hidden in my life.
- ❑ I will understand that my only hope is in complete dependence on God and obedience to Him.

SCRIPTURES:

Proverbs 8:13 (NLT)
All who fear the LORD will hate evil. Therefore, I hate pride and arrogance, corruption and perverse speech.

Proverbs 13:10 (NLT)
Pride leads to conflict; those who take advice are wise.

1 Peter 5:6 (NLT)
So humble yourselves under the mighty power of God, and at the right time he will lift you up in honor.

Philippians 2:3 (NLT)
Don't be selfish; don't try to impress others. Be humble, thinking of others as better than yourselves.

Philippians 2:4 (NLT)
Don't look out only for your own interests, but take an interest in others, too.

Colossians 3: 12 (NLT)
Since God chose you to be the holy people he loves, you must clothe yourselves with tenderhearted mercy, kindness, humility, gentleness, and patience.

NOTES:

Webster's Dictionary defines "rebellion" as: 1) an act or state of armed, open resistance to authority, government, etc.; 2) defiance of or opposition to any control.

1 Samuel 15:22–23 (NKJV) *So Samuel said: "Has the Lord as great delight in burnt offerings and sacrifices, as in obeying the voice of the Lord? Behold, to obey is better than sacrifice, and to heed than the fat of rams. For **rebellion is as the sin of witchcraft**, and stubbornness is as iniquity and idolatry. Because you have rejected the word of the Lord, He also has rejected you from being king."*

King Saul and Rebellion

The above verses, 1 Samuel 15: 22–23, are the account of King Saul operating in a self-willed way so that he disregarded God's directives to him and operated in self-determination. These actions actually were partial obedience to God's directives, but partial obedience is disobedience and disobedience is rebellion.

This was not the first time for King Saul. He had developed a pattern of disregarding God and His directives, of generally obeying as God directed but according to his own level of comfort, wisdom, and convenience.

Even though Saul was king over Israel, he was under the authority of Another, whose plans and instructions were revealed through the prophet Samuel. Perhaps Saul thought, *Just this once won't matter; after all, who does Samuel think he is?* Saul's rebellion and self-will, however, caused him to go against the word of the Lord.

Finally, God could no longer spare His mercy toward Saul's rebellion. Consequently, Samuel, speaking on behalf of God called out King Saul on his rebellion. Samuel, in faithfulness to God, told King Saul, *"Rebellion is as the sin of witchcraft."* Rebellion places you in Satan's realm. Satan's domain was built on rebellion; his kingdom is a kingdom of rebellion.

The result was a judgment like that of Satan. Samuel went on to say that God had rejected Saul from being king. His dynasty was ripped from Saul's family. Saul's life had a terrible demise, ending in the loss of his sons in battle. Seeing his own life about ready to end in humiliation and suffering at the hands of his enemies, he committed suicide.

Thoughts on Pride

Pride causes us to think and to feel that we are independent. It sets us up as "rebels" against God and His authority. Satan set up a heavenly rebellion against God and His authority, and it is believed by many Bible students that he convinced one third of the angels to follow him in that rebellion (Revelation 12:4). Isaiah 14 makes it clear that Satan was given a free will and exercised it five times, stating, "I will" against the established authority of God. God's response to Satan and those with him was to hurl them out of heaven to earth. (Isaiah 14:13–14)

Like Satan, we also have been given a free will with the ability to choose our own way. We too can rebel against God or choose to submit to His established authority.

Jesus stated: *"Those who obey My commandments are the ones who love Me. And because they love Me, My Father will love them, and I will love them. And I will reveal myself to each one of them."* (John 14:21) Jesus commanded those of us who know and identify with Him to live a life consistent with the character of Christ and bear the fruits of righteousness.

Christ always lived and carried out His ministry "according to the will of the Father." Jesus was characterized by humility. He followed at all times the Father's direction, will, and authority. Even in death, Jesus was heard saying, "Not My will, but Yours be done."

Rebellion utterly destroys one's life. "Fruits" of rebellion include:

- Designating ourselves as the supreme authority
- Aligning ourselves with the foundation of Satan's kingdom
- Resisting and rebelling against parents, spouses, civil authorities, social authorities (bosses, teachers, etc.), and spiritual authorities (pastors, elders, ministry leaders, etc.)

- Regarding others from a "who do they think they are?" point of view
- Elevating your own will above Scripture, above authorities in your life, above the laws of your government
- Lives and structures that are overrun by chaos, disorder, confusion, and revolution
- Insubordination to authority

Rebellion expresses itself in:

- Critical speech against those in authority
- Lies
- Anger, bitterness, rage
- Loading up others with guilt
- Manipulating others so as to get one's own way
- Division and divisiveness
- Open revolution against established authority
- Covert or overt disobedience
- Willingness and/or efforts to discredit those in authority
- Passive and open resistance to particular people in authority or to any established authority structure

RECOGNIZING REBELLION

- ❑ I find it difficult to accept others' leadership easily.
- ❑ I often speak or think critically of those who are in positions of authority.
- ❑ I often feel "something rise up within me" when I am asked or told to do something with which I don't agree.
- ❑ I often try to influence others to see established authority in a negative light.
- ❑ I do not view my response to human authorities in my life as a response to God.
- ❑ I often think and feel that I could do a better job than those who are in authority are doing.

- ❑ I find it easy to excuse and justify my disobedience to authority.
- ❑ I engage in speech that criticizes or discredits those in authority.
- ❑ I would rather believe "hearsay" about those in authority than seek the truth from those in authority.
- ❑ I try to manipulate those in authority over me so as to get my own way.
- ❑ I find ways to "get around" obeying what those in authority ask of me.
- ❑ I use religious and spiritual actions and involvement to mask disobedience, self-will, and insubordination.
- ❑ I try to influence others to side with me against those in authority.
- ❑ My life tends to be marked by or known for chaos, disorder, anger, rage, or being critical.
- ❑ It seems that nothing ever goes right for me.

The core of rebellion is to set us against God, and God views rebellion as a very grievous issue. Rebellion gives Satan and his kingdom a foothold in our lives, and places us under his jurisdiction. We also open ourselves up to the judgment of God.

Living a Life of Submission

Even Jesus was submissive and obedient to those God had placed in authority over Him. His entire life was submission; during His earthly ministry, everything He did and said was done according to the will of the Father, up to and including His death.

We can covenant with the Lord to begin walking according to His will, dying to ourselves, and submitting cheerfully those the Lord has placed in authority over us. Realize that <u>He</u> has placed those in authority over us in their positions. By obeying and submitting to them, we are obeying and submitting to God! Get this: <u>one cannot be rebellious toward human authority without being rebellious toward God.</u>

THE 4 Rs FOR REBELLION

REPENTANCE

Take responsibility for rebellion and specifically the ways you have acted out rebellion.

Sample Prayer: *Lord, I repent of the sin of rebellion. I confess right now that I have allowed it to become a part of my life. I call it out before You as sin. I break off rebellion in any area of my life right now by turning in the opposite direction and living a life of submission and obedience to You, Your Word, and Your ways, and human authorities You have put in my life.*

REBUKE

Renounce every lie concerning your right to live rebellious and rebuke every spirit that you have allowed to empower rebellion in your life.

Sample Prayer: *I rebuke and bind the lies of the enemy right now. Their attack on my life in the area of rebellion is broken. I rebuke every evil spirit that has empowered the stronghold of rebellion in my life. I will not give you a place in my life through rebellion. I command you to the feet of Jesus to receive His judgment for you.*

REPLACE

It takes an absolute hatred for the sin of rebellion in order to walk free of it. It is a deep cleansing of part of your personality, including your ways of thinking, your reactions, and your motives. Acknowledge and affirm that you will live in submission and obedience to God and authorities He has put in your life. Be as specific in your declaration of replacement as your were in your attitude and actions of rebellion.

Sample Prayer: *I right now declare by God's grace that I will live in such a way as to trust God with my life. I trust Him with my well-being and my future. I will submit to God and to others who are authorities in my life in specific attitudes and actions of submission and obedience.*

RECEIVE

Request and receive the filling of the Holy Spirit to fill every place that was once inhabited by the sin of rebellion. Thank the Lord that He has totally forgiven you. Receive His full cleansing and rejoice.

Sample Prayer: *Lord, fill me with Your Holy Spirit that I may live supernaturally in the freedom of faith and trust in You in submission and obedience. I receive Your forgiveness for the sin of rebellion in my life. I receive Your love for me.*

WALKING IN THE OPPOSITE SPIRIT

To walk in the opposite spirit of rebellion, determine to grow in the "character of Christ" and cultivate these habits of a submissive spirit in your life:

- ☐ I will live in submission to those God has placed in authority over me, with the understanding that in doing so I am submitting to God.

- ☐ I will understand that all those who have authority—whether civil, social, family, or church—have been placed in those positions by God.

- ☐ I will live in a manner that respects and submits to others.

- ☐ I will understand that a spirit of submission and obedience enlarges my capacity for God to move freely, fully, and powerfully in and through my life.

- ☐ I will honor those in authority; I will seek to support them and protect their honor.

Don't forget this:

Working through the evidence of rebellion in us is essential if we are to live a life of joyful submission to God. We cannot expect to receive God's blessings and favor without exchanging our rebellion for a spirit of submission to Him.

SCRIPTURES:

Matthew 22:37
And He said to him, "You shall love the Lord your God with all your heart, and with all your soul, and with all your mind."

Hebrews 5:7–8
During the days of Jesus' life on earth, he offered up prayers and petitions with loud cries and tears to the one who could save him from death, and he was heard because of his reverent submission. Although he was a son, he learned obedience from what he suffered.

John 5:30
By myself I can do nothing; I judge only as I hear, and my judgment is just, for I seek not to please myself but him who sent me.

Matthew 26:39
Going a little farther, he fell with his face to the ground and prayed, "My Father, if it is possible, may this cup be taken from me. Yet not as I will, but as you will."

Isaiah 63:9–10
In all their distress he too was distressed, and the angel of his presence saved them. In his love and mercy he redeemed them; he lifted them up and carried them all the days of old. Yet they rebelled and grieved his Holy Spirit. So he turned and became their enemy and he himself fought against them.

1 Samuel 12:15
But if you do not obey the Lord, and if you rebel against his commands, his hand will be against you, as it was against your fathers. Joshua 1:18 "Whoever rebels against your word and does not obey your words, whatever you may command them, will be put to death. Only be strong and courageous!"

Ezekiel 3:7
But the house of Israel is not willing to listen to you because they are not willing to listen to me, for the whole house of Israel is hardened and obstinate.

Romans 13:1–2
Everyone must submit himself to the governing authorities, for there is no authority except that which God has established. The authorities that exist have been established by God. Consequently, he who rebels against the authority is rebelling against what God has instituted, and those who do so will bring judgment on themselves.

Hebrews 13:17
Obey your leaders and submit to them, for they keep watch over your souls as those who will give an account. Let them do this with joy and not with grief, for this would be unprofitable for you.

1 Peter 2:13–14, 17
Submit yourselves for the Lord's sake to every human institution, whether to a king as the one in authority, or to governors as sent by him for the punishment of evildoers and the praise of those who do right. Honor all people, love the brotherhood, fear God, honor the king.

Romans 13:1
Everyone must submit himself to the governing authorities, for there is no authority except that which God has established. The authorities that exist have been established by God.

2 Peter 1:3
His divine power has given us everything we need for life and godliness through our knowledge of him who called us by his own glory and goodness.

REJECTION

> A pattern of feeling disregarded, rebuffed, slighted, unloved, and undesired by God and people with a deep-seated fear that you cannot live a life of approval.

We belong to a society that values winning and worships winners. We live under a world system that chooses favorites and rejects seconds. We learn, practically from birth, that the most popular, the most attractive, and the most talented are "in." Those who don't fit that description (most of us) are "out." And so, before even a particular action or attitude is leveled against us, the stage is set for each of us to live life battling rejection.

Biblical Examples

The biblical examples are prolific men and women existing in a context of rejection. Hagar (Sarah's handmaiden), Noah, Joseph, Samuel, David, Jeremiah, the woman at the well, and, not the least, Jesus Himself.

The classic Old Testament character who experienced rejection is Joseph. Many see Joseph as a preview of Jesus in the context of rejection. Joseph was set apart by God as was Jesus; Joseph had received specific revelation from God as did Jesus; born out of jealousy, Joseph was rejected by his family, as was Jesus. Joseph's brothers sold him into slavery that separated him from his family, homeland, and culture (Genesis 37).

Sadly, Joseph's master and boss Potiphar rewarded Joseph's integrity and loyalty with rejection and betrayal. Joseph fled to resist Potiphar's wife's seduction to engage in sexual immoralities with her. His boss subsequently assigned him to the rigors of an ancient Egyptian prison.

Joseph overcame these rejections. He prevailed and lived beyond rejection and victimization. Joseph became one who protected, provided, and blessed his family. He was his family's savior. Without him, they very well might not have survived while they were living in a widespread famine (Genesis 42–50). He was liberated through the power of forgiveness and found security in his life and purpose in God.

God also used Joseph to save a world from famine and death. They key that allowed him to live with competence, divine wisdom, and leadership was forgiveness.

We see another example of rejection experienced in the life of Hagar, Sarah's servant maid. Genesis 16 tells us that Sarah schemed for Abraham to have a son by Hagar to provide God's promise for a son. Hagar conceived and gave birth to Ishmael.

Genesis 21 describes Hagar being actively rejected by Sarah and by Abraham. Hagar was cast out from Abraham's family, and in isolation struggled to exist in a desolate desert with her young son.

It is hard to imagine the extent of her confusion, wounds, fear, and heartache. Rejection is brutally painful to experience, and most often affects a people for long periods of time, if not a lifetime.

Insights to Rejection

Rejection is foundational to many strongholds, sins, and dysfunctions. This foundational consequence is that rejection affects a person's entire personality. It not only works against an individual, but it works against all of a person's relationships: marriage, family, ministry, work, and social life. When each of us begins to make our way in life, the stage is already set by the world system, which we know to be under the direction of Satan, the "accuser of the brethren" (Revelation 12:10). Where we yearn for love and acceptance, we often receive rejection instead. We learn to believe the lies fed to us about our value, our significance, and God's love, our Heavenly Father.

However, if we are in Christ, we do not need to participate in this world system. Rejection is not our inheritance; we have been accepted (Romans 15:7). There is nothing that can separate us from the love of our Father (Romans 8:38–39), and we must not buy into the lies that tell us otherwise. Instead, we must face those lies squarely, identify what they are and where they come from, and destroy them utterly with the sword of the Spirit—which is the Word of God.

POTENTIAL ROOTS OF REJECTION

- ❑ Absent fathers or mothers
- ❑ Lack of bonding with parents
- ❑ Parents' divorce
- ❑ Not being wanted as a child
- ❑ Being told you are the "wrong" gender
- ❑ Adoption
- ❑ Competition with siblings
- ❑ Various forms of abuse (physical, emotional, sexual)
- ❑ Parents' addictions
- ❑ Shame of a family member
- ❑ Constant fighting or strife
- ❑ Disinterest in your activities and interests as a child or adult
- ❑ Various means and degrees of neglect/abandonment
- ❑ Living with physical defect or handicap
- ❑ Breaking off an engagement or other significant relationship
- ❑ Infidelity of a spouse
- ❑ Divorce
- ❑ Loss of valued employment
- ❑ Betrayal by a loyal friend
- ❑ Spiritual abuse, hurt, or betrayal in a church
- ❑ Unjust discipline
- ❑ Racial prejudices
- ❑ Class distinctions

DIAGNOSTIC QUESTIONS

Please check any boxes you feel may apply to you.

My Mindset:

- ❏ I usually interpret things that could be either positive or negative as negative.

- ❏ I have negative thoughts about what others must think about me as a result of my words or actions.

- ❏ I get assaulted with paralyzing thoughts of how others feel about me.

- ❏ I don't believe people when they pay me a compliment.

- ❏ I tend to be skeptical and unbelieving of other peoples' overtures of friendship or appreciation.

- ❏ I do not share my testimony, or the gospel, with people due to fear of rejection.

- ❏ I do not step out in ministry toward others due to fear of rejection.

- ❏ I relate to people in pride, egotism, and arrogance.

- ❏ I am compelled to reject others.

- ❏ I tend toward harshness, skepticism, and unbelief.

- ❏ I live with self-rejection evidenced in low self-image, inferiority, insecurity, inadequacy, sorrow, and grief.

- ❏ I battle self-destructive thoughts and actions.

- ❏ I live life in over-achievement, striving, competition, and perfectionism.

- ❏ I struggle with depression, hopelessness, and despair.

- ❏ I am more comfortable living in withdrawal, isolation, or independence.

- ❏ I tend to be critical, judgmental, and jealous/envious.

- ❏ I have a low estimation of my appearance, my abilities, and my adequacy to succeed in life and ministry.

My Actions:

- ☐ I find it difficult to freely reach out and exercise my passions and gifts in ministry for fear of how they will be received.

- ☐ I often try to "do too much" or go from thing to thing, job to job, ministry to ministry, striving to earn favor and acceptance from God and/or others.

- ☐ I find it difficult to accept freely from others, or to demonstrate love and affection.

- ☐ I tend to doubt, question, or mistrust authority.

- ☐ People could describe me as harsh.

- ☐ I struggle to control foul language and abusive speech, especially when I am angry.

- ☐ I rely on coping mechanisms (false comforts), instead of on the truth, power, and strength of God's Holy Spirit.

- ☐ I struggle with rebellion, aggressive attitudes, foul language, stubbornness, defiance, fighting, and abusive actions.

- ☐ I find that I struggle with control, manipulation, and possessiveness.

- ☐ I am prone toward self-accusation and self-condemnation.

- ☐ I live through the lens of performance-based life in relationships and ministry.

- ☐ I need to be needed, so I continually place myself in situations where I feel others cannot get along without my help, my presence, my abilities, my ministries, etc.

- ☐ I am possessive in relationships.

My Responses:

- ☐ My immediate reaction is defensive or even defiant when confronted about something.

- ☐ When people say nice things to me, I wonder what they actually think.

- ☐ When I find myself in conflict with another, it is easier for me to distance myself in the relationship and reject that person than work through the issue.

- ☐ My relationships feed fears, anxieties, worries, negativity, and pessimism.

- ☐ I respond to people in self-protection, self-centeredness, selfishness, self-justification, and self-pity (it's all about SELF!).

- ❑ I find it difficult to accept from others freely, or to demonstrate love and affection.

- ❑ I feel comfort in isolation—others might consider me a loner.

- ❑ I am both critical and envious at the same time toward others who are more confident who can express themselves freely, or who have more friendships and opportunities than I think I do.

- ❑ I am inhibited in honestly sharing my deepest feelings with others, even with those who are close to me.

THE 4 Rs FOR REJECTION

REPENTANCE:

1. Grant forgiveness to those from whom you have felt the pain of rejection. Grant forgiveness to any organization or people in whom you have experienced the hurt of rejection. Forgive them for how they made you feel, and how they specifically rejected and hurt you. Give up any unforgiveness and resentment.

2. SPECIFICALLY, BLESS THEM!

3. Though you may feel rejected because of wounds or injustices from the past, what we want to look at here is any sinful ways you might have responded. For example, you may need to confess the sin of living self-focused, with self-protection, anger, isolation, false comforts, resentment, unforgiveness, or not believing what God says is true about you. You may need to confess the sin of not receiving the love Jesus died to give you. Repent of living as one spurned or rejected when the Lord of the Universe has chosen you to love you.

Sample Prayer: *Lord, I have consistently thought of what others think of me, worrying that I will not be approved. I have not believed that Your acceptance was of great and sustaining value. I have not believed that You accept me with joy and that You even delight in me. I have hurt others by rejecting them first because I feared they would reject me. I have not forgiven those who rejected me and have held onto my pain. I have isolated myself and been independent of others to protect my feelings. I have even refused to obey You for fear of other people's rejection. These are my sins, and I ask You to forgive me, Lord.*

REBUKE

Resist the evil spirits of rejection, who have assaulted your mind with lies about who you are and how others or God feel about you. Renounce these lies and command the evil spirits of rejection to go to the feet of Jesus.

Sample Prayer: *By the authority of my Savior, Jesus Christ, I renounce every lie of the enemy against me. I renounce the lie that I am rejected. I renounce the lie that others will always reject me. I renounce the lie that I must hold onto hurt to protect myself. I renounce the lie that I must prove myself through accomplishments to others and to God. I command every deceiving, condemning spirit of rejection to be gone right now in the name of Jesus Christ. Go to the feet of Jesus to receive your judgment.*

REPLACE

Replace fear of rejection with confident assurance in the love of Christ. Replace self-doubt with the truth that you are a chosen vessel, the beloved of Christ. Replace self-pity with the joy of being called and empowered to do Kingdom work for the King of kings. Write a list of affirmations based on the Scriptures of use the following to take a firm stand against the stronghold of rejection.

Sample Prayer: *Lord, by Your grace, I believe, declare, and will live in the reality of Your love and acceptance of me. I will live recognizing that You celebrate me and that You delight in every detail of my life. The knowledge of Your truth and regard for me will take priority over how others may treat or relate to me. I will freely and fully love others knowing that I am infinitely accepted and loved by You.*

RECEIVE

Thank God that He fully accepts you through the blood of Christ. Thank Him for freely forgiving you. Ask for and receive the filling of God's Holy Spirit.

Sample Prayer: *Holy Spirit, fill me with Your presence and power, so that I might live the supernatural life; living life in the knowledge that my Heavenly Father fully accepts me. His acceptance fulfills and satisfies me. Fill with me with Your power to relate to others, so they experience full acceptance and love from You through me. You have accepted me, and I thank You that even now You open Your arms to receive me. I receive Your love and forgiveness.*

WALKING IN THE OPPOSITE SPIRIT

When we are faced with the fear of rejection, the temptation is to fall back on coping mechanisms we may have employed for most—if not all—of our lives. These can include anything we have learned to use or to do to comfort ourselves in the face of rejection or other hurts. We should recognize our coping mechanisms as "false comforts"; like a placebo, they trick us into thinking we've dealt with the symptoms of our pain when in truth they do nothing to solve the problem.

- ❏ I will no longer seek comfort in self-pity or isolation.
- ❏ I will treat other people according to the truth of God's Word, not on the basis of my own fears, hurts, and insecurities. I will forgive. I will extend blessing. I will freely love and accept others.
- ❏ I will express my thoughts and feelings to others honestly without fear of rejection.
- ❏ I will no longer resort to rebellion to express my anger over feeling rejected.
- ❏ I will cease to try to "do" for others so that they will love and accept me. I will minister with my spiritual gifts according to the direction and power of the Holy Spirit.
- ❏ I will not be critical of those I feel have rejected me, or those whom I regard as walking in greater freedom, acceptance, or confidence than me.
- ❏ I will form attitudes, initiate actions, and speak words that will comfort and encourage others.
- ❏ I will "be myself," enjoying and becoming more comfortable with how God made me.

SCRIPTURES:

Isaiah 41:9–10 *You whom I have taken from the ends of the earth and called from its remotest parts and said to you, 'You are My servant, I have chosen you and not rejected you. 'Do not fear, for I am with you; Do not anxiously look about you, for I am your God and I will strengthen you, surely I will help you, Surely I will uphold you with my Righteous right hand.'*

Isaiah 53:3 *He was despised and forsaken of men, A man of sorrows and acquainted with grief; and like one from whom men hide their face He was despised, and we did not esteem Him.*

Psalm 27:1,10 *The Lord is my light and my salvation; whom shall I fear? The Lord is the defense of my life; whom shall I dread? For my father and my mother have forsaken me, but the Lord will take me up.*

Isaiah 62:3–4 *You will also be a crown of beauty in the hand of the Lord, and a royal diadem in the hand of your God. It will no longer be said to you "Forsaken," Nor to your land will it any longer be said, "Desolate;" but you will be called, "My delight is in her," and your land, "Married;" For the Lord delights in you, and to Him your land will be married.*

1 Peter 2:4–5 *And coming to Him as to a living stone which has been rejected by men but is a choice and precious in the sight of God, you also, as living stones, are being built up as a spiritual house for a holy priesthood, to offer up spiritual sacrifices acceptable to God through Jesus Christ.*

1 John 3:1 *See how great a love the Father has bestowed on us, that we would be called children of God; and such we are!*

RELIGIOUS SPIRIT

> The religious spirit seeks to prevent, stop, or distort a genuine work or move of God through deception, control, and manipulation.

In Matthew 5:20 Jesus told His disciples that if their righteousness did not exceed that of the religious leaders of His day, they could not enter the Kingdom of Heaven. The Scribes and Pharisees had made a religion out of their traditions, making God's Word of no effect, yet attributing their activity to God.

A religious spirit presents itself in many forms and expressions. Quite honestly, most everyone is susceptible to living in and out of a religious spirit.

Pharisees

The religious Pharisees of the New Testament, with whom Jesus battled, were concerned with outward appearances and the rules of their religious culture. They wanted all to see their actions and deeds while their hearts were far from God and His people. They enjoyed having a title and being recognized, always feeding the flesh of self-righteousness. They went through outward cleansing but neglected the most important cleansing, which was their heart. They loved to bind people to their laws of tradition rather than setting them free! They made disciples after their own ideas and hidden agendas, bringing death instead of life (Matthew 23). Jesus had very stern words for them.

The Galatian Believers

In the New Testament, the Galatians started their Christian life simply by believing and having faith in God. However, somewhere along the road, they were influenced to live their lives by focusing on rules and regulations and living according to their own human effort. Read the apostle Paul's words as he confronted the believers in Galatia about the effect of the religious spirit in their lives in Galatians 3:1–5.

> *You foolish Galatians! Who has bewitched you? Before your very eyes, Jesus Christ was clearly portrayed as crucified. I would like to learn just one thing from you: Did you receive the Spirit by observing the law, or by believing what you heard? Are you so foolish? After beginning with the Spirit, are you now trying to attain your goal by human effort? Have you suffered so much for nothing–if it really was for nothing? Does God give you his Spirit and work miracles among you because you observe the law, or because you believe what you heard?*

Living according to rules and regulations and by our own human efforts is a trap set by the religious spirit into which we can fall. However, it is not the abundant life that Jesus promised in John 10:10.

The Rich Young Ruler

In the Gospel of Matthew, we also read about a rich young ruler who could not commit to the one true God because of the religious spirit. Although he considered himself religious because he followed the laws, he had an idol in his life that prevented him from making a total or "sold-out" commitment to Jesus (Matthew 19:16–22).

The rich young ruler wanted to gain God's approval on his own terms by fulfilling the law. However, Jesus cut through the religious spirit by speaking to the heart of his issue.

King Saul

King Saul in the Old Testament was very religious in calling fasts and public gatherings of worship while at the same time living in self-willed religion and rebellion. His religious activities were efforts to compensate for his sin.

Thoughts on the Religious Spirit

These are but a few of the many examples of the religious spirit in action in the Scriptures. Satan is always out to prevent a true work of God in people's personal lives and communities.

The religious spirit is divisive, destructive, and brings death. It divides the body of Christ and separates His people from God's life and freedom. It seeks to prevent genuine, powerful movements of God. It is always working against God's Kingdom.

The religious spirit has many faces. It is very deceptive in taking on a persona of religion and light, but it is evil and dark. It is a spirit that is assigned to distract people from the truth by making people think that they are okay or deceiving them into thinking they have the corner on the market of truth.

The spirit of religion is the meanest, foulest, most malevolent spirit that you will ever confront. It comes as an impostor, masquerading as the real thing but cutting off believers from a relationship with God and blocking the work of the Holy Spirit.

With the religious spirit, you will always find a judgmental and critical spirit, pride, legalism, formalism, error, control, bondages, and manipulation, just to name a few characteristics!

It is one of Satan's greatest weapons against the people of God. It will lull them into slumber and apathy, making them numb and ineffective in the work of the Kingdom. When religion reigns, it has a form of godliness but will deny or thwart God's power.

The religious spirit also attacks those who are working in God's Kingdom. It has a venomous hatred for those truly doing God's work. It accused Jesus of casting out devils by the devil (Matt.9:34). It killed God's prophets in the Old Testament, along with John the Baptist and Stephen in the New Testament.

When people get freedom and release from religion and all the supporting lying spirits, people can then be filled with Truth and the Holy Spirit! They will begin to produce life-giving fruit! They will enter God's abundant life. We need to examine ourselves and see if this spirit has infiltrated our hearts at any level.

Christians should ask themselves a few questions. *Am I more concerned about rules than relationship? Have I settled for not seeing and operating in God's power? Do I walk in the love of the Father for people? Do I desire to be a part of a "good show" gospel rather than a biblical gospel?* Religion can and will be very subtle as it slips in to find a seat in our heart!

One of the greatest weapons against it is to be like Jesus. We also must prioritize intimacy with the Lord and allow our lives to flow out of that relationship. Our prayer should be that our eyes, where they were blinded by religion, would opened to see the deception of the enemy, and that our understanding would be enlightened so that freedom could come. Paul explicitly warns that the devil, by his craftiness, can corrupt minds and keep them from "the simplicity that is in Christ" (2 Corinthians 11:3).

RELIGIOUS SPIRIT DIAGNOSTIC

Go through the warning signs below and check the ways you may be operating out of a religious spirit in that area of your life. Remember that unconditional love can only win this battle, a life focused on Jesus, the Word of God, and being filled with the Holy Spirit. So, use this checklist to set yourself free to worship, walk, and work with the Holy Spirit.

- ❑ **The tendency to see your primary mission as tearing down what you believe is wrong.** This person's ministry will produce more division than lasting works.

- ❑ **The inability to take a rebuke, especially from those you judge to be less spiritual than yourself.** Think back on how you responded the last few times someone tried to correct you.

- ❑ **A mindset that will not listen to other people—"only to God."** This is arrogant and delusional, setting you up for deception and isolation.

- ❑ **The inclination to see more of what is wrong with other people and other churches than what is right with them.**

- ❑ **Overwhelming guilt that you can never measure up to the Lord's standards.** This is a root of the religious spirit because it causes you to base your relationship with Him on your performance rather than on the cross.

- ❑ **The belief that you have been appointed to fix everyone else!** To be self-appointed and self-righteous is living in a self-delusional way that allows you to think you are closer to God than others or that your life or ministry is more pleasing to Him.

- ❑ **A leadership style that is bossy, overbearing and intolerant of the failure of others.** As James said: "But the wisdom from above is first pure, then peaceable, gentle, reasonable, full of mercy and good fruits, unwavering, without hypocrisy. And the seed whose fruit is righteousness is sown in peace by those who make peace" (James 3:17–18).

- ❑ **Pride in your spiritual maturity or discipline, especially as you compare yourself to others.**

- ❑ **The belief that you are on the cutting edge of what God is doing.** This includes thinking that you are involved in the most important thing that God is doing.

- ❑ **A mechanical prayer life.** When you start feeling relieved that your prayer time is over, or when you have prayed though your prayer list, you should check your condition.

- ❑ **Doing things so people will notice.**

- ❑ **Being overly repulsed by emotionalism.** When people who are subject to a religious spirit encounter the true life of God, it will usually appear excessive and demonstrative to them. Remember how David danced when he brought the ark of the God into Jerusalem? This repulsed his wife Michal and she was barren from that day on (2 Samuel 6:23). Such a critical spirit will lead to spiritual barrenness.

- ❑ **Using emotionalism as a substitute for the work of the Holy Spirit.** Do you think that weeping and wailing must accompany repentance? Or, that you must be over-demonstrative or loud (attracting attention to yourself), or that one must "fall under the power" to be truly touched by God (or jerk, or any other behaviorism)? Even though some of these can be evidences of the true work of the Holy Spirit, you are beginning to move in another spirit if you seek after these manifestations instead of seeking intimacy with Jesus.

- ❑ (During Jonathon Edward's meetings in the First Great Awakening some of the toughest, most rebellious men fell on the ground and stayed there for up to 24 hours.

Such seemingly strange manifestations fueled the Great Awakening, since these men were truly changed. Even so, Edwards stated men who faked these manifestations brought an end to the Great Awakening more than the enemies of the revival.)

- **Keeping score in your spiritual life.** Do you feel better about yourself because you go to more meetings, read your Bible more, or do more things for the Lord than other people do?

- **Being encouraged when your ministry looks better than others' ministries.**

- **Glorying more in what God has done in the past than what He is doing in the present.** A religious spirit always seeks to focus our attention on making comparisons rather than simply drawing closer to Jesus.

- **The tendency to be suspicious of or oppose new movements or churches.** This is an obvious symptom of jealousy, a primary fruit of the religious spirit.

- **The tendency to reject spiritual manifestations that we do not understand.** This is a symptom of pride and arrogance that presumes our opinions are the same as God's. True humility keeps us teachable and open, patiently waiting for fruit before making judgments.

- **An overreaction to immaturity in the church.**

- **The inability to join anything that you do not deem as being perfect or near perfect.**

- **If while reading theses signs you were thinking about how they applied to someone else, you may have a serious problem with a religious spirit.**

SOME FORMS OF A RELIGIOUS SPIRIT

The following are four forms of a religious spirit:

The Counterfeit Gift of Discernment

A religious spirit gives birth to a counterfeit gift of discernment of spirits. This counterfeit gift thrives on seeing what is wrong with others rather than seeing what God is doing to help them along. Though the discernment may be accurate, it is ministered in a spirit that kills.

Suspicion, which is motivated by rejection, territorial preservation, or general insecurity, causes this counterfeit gift. However, the true gift of discernment can only function with love. In 2 Corinthians 11:13–15, Paul warns his readers about those who minister in a religious spirit, that they try to place a yoke of legalism on the believers.

The Spirit of Jezebel

The Spirit of Jezebel is a combination of the religious spirit and the spirit of witchcraft that is the spirit of manipulation and control (as demonstrated by Queen Jezebel in 1 and 2 Kings). This spirit will be characterized by a religious rebellion, deception, and manipulation. It also will use sensual deception and temptation in its efforts to compromise God's work and God's people (again as demonstrated by Queen Jezebel).

The Jezebel spirit is one of the enemy's most potent forms of the religious spirit that seeks to compromise God's people and Kingdom work. This spirit attacks the prophetic ministry (as Jezebel did against Elijah) through which the Lord wants to give timely, strategic direction to His people. Jezebel knows that by removing the true prophets, the people will be vulnerable to her false prophets. When there is a void of the true prophetic word, the people will be much more prone to the deception of the enemy.

This religious spirit seeks to kill God's work and His people (as demonstrated by Queen Jezebel).

Self-Righteousness

We do not crucify ourselves for the sake of righteousness, purification, and spiritual maturity or to get the Lord to manifest Himself; this is nothing less than conjuring. We are "crucified with Christ" by faith (Galatians 2:20). If we crucify ourselves, it will only result in self-righteousness. This is pride in its most base form because it gives the appearance of wisdom and righteousness.

In Colossians 2:18–23, Paul warns us of pride, about focusing on how well we are doing compared to others and not for God's glory. This results in our putting confidence in discipline and personal sacrifice rather than in the Lord and His sacrifice. It is the motivation behind everything we do that is important—driven by the Holy Spirit or a religious spirit. A religious spirit motivates through fear, guilt, or pride and ambition. The Holy Spirit motivates through love for Jesus Christ.

In Colossians 2:16–23, Paul explains that people who delight in self-abasement will often be given to worshiping angels and taking improper stands on visions they have seen. A religious spirit wants us to worship anything or anyone but Jesus. God does not give us revelations to prove our ministry or so people will respect us more. The fruit of true revelation will be humility not pride. A religious spirit will always feed our pride, whereas true spiritual maturity will always lead to increasing humility.

The Martyr Syndrome

To be a true martyr for the faith is one of the greatest honors that we can receive in this life. When this is perverted, it is a tragic form of deception. At that point, any rejection or correction is perceived as the price one must bear to "stand for the truth" which drives a person even farther from the truth and any possibility of correction.

THE 4 Rs FOR THE RELIGIOUS SPIRIT

REPENTANCE

Take responsibility for the religious spirit in your life by confessing specifically the sin of trusting in yourself and human efforts to live out God's life. Confess any pride and/or self-righteousness that would accompany the religious spirit. Use the diagnostic list on page 94 so your confession and repentance can be specific.

> **Sample Prayer:** *Lord, I repent of the sin of the false religious spirit and associated activities (be specific at this point). I confess right now that I have allowed it to become a part of my life. I call it out before You as sin. I break the control of this religious spirit in my life right now by turning in the opposite direction and living a life of trust in and yielding to You, Your Word, and Your ways by your Holy Spirit.*

REBUKE

Renounce every lie you have held onto related to the religious spirit. In the authority of Jesus Christ, resist Satan and any evil spirits that have found a place to empower false spirituality in your life.

> **Sample Prayer:** *I rebuke and bind the lies of the enemy right now and their attack on my life in false spirituality in a religious spirit. I sever all ties to the stronghold of the religious spirit in my life. I rebuke every evil spirit that has empowered false religion in my life. I command you to the feet of Jesus to receive His judgment.*

REPLACE

It takes an absolute hatred for the sin of false spirituality in the religious spirit to walk free of it. It is a deep cleansing of part of your personality, including your ways of thinking, your actions, and your motives. Use "Walking in the Opposite Spirit" checklist on page 99 to help you identify the truth, motive, and action that will oppose the sin, and make a declaration that will characterize you by God's grace.

> **Sample Prayer:** *I right now declare by God's grace that I will live in simple, humble obedience to God and to be Christlike in my attitudes, motives, and actions. Where there was religious pride*

I will be humble. I will replace religious rigidity and its self-righteousness with a teachable spirit. I will live so as to keep in step with the Spirit. (Be specific in your declaration of replacement.)

RECEIVE

Request and receive the filling of the Holy Spirit to fill every place that was once inhabited by false spirituality of the religious spirit. Thank the Lord that He has totally forgiven you. Receive His full cleansing and rejoice.

Sample Prayer: *Lord, fill me with Your Holy Spirit that I may live supernaturally in the freedom of Your truth and Holy Spirit. I receive Your love for me.*

WALKING IN THE OPPOSITE SPIRIT

- ❏ I will build up those around me and speak that which will strengthen, encourage, and edify.
- ❏ I will be open to receive godly, love-filled input and correction so that I might grow into greater Christlikeness and fruitfulness.
- ❏ I will work at seeing what is right and good in people and ministries and to pray for them instead of being critical and tearing them down.
- ❏ I will increasingly live in God's grace and relate to others in His grace.
- ❏ When I can minister, lead, and exercise responsibility I will do so in a servant-like spirit.
- ❏ I will compare my life and ministry to that of Jesus Christ and Him alone.
- ❏ I will celebrate the work that God is doing in others to advance His Kingdom.
- ❏ I will gladly serve in a way as to be nameless and faceless in humility and not be motivated by the recognition of people.
- ❏ I will measure my spiritual life not by my spiritual disciplines and works but by my love for Jesus and desired intimacy with my Heavenly Father.
- ❏ I will be teachable and open to new expressions of God in my life and that of others.

SCRIPTURES:

1 Samuel 15:22 (NLT)
But Samuel replied, "What is more pleasing to the LORD: your burnt offerings and sacrifices or your obedience to his voice? Listen! Obedience is better than sacrifice, and submission is better than offering the fat of rams.

Psalm 51:16–17 (NLT)
You do not desire a sacrifice, or I would offer one. You do not want a burnt offering. 17 The sacrifice you desire is a broken spirit. You will not reject a broken and repentant heart, O God.

Micah 6:6–8 (NLT)
What can we bring to the LORD? Should we bring him burnt offerings? Should we bow before God Most High with offerings of yearling calves? 7 Should we offer him thousands of rams and ten thousand rivers of olive oil? Should we sacrifice our firstborn children to pay for our sins? 8 No, O people, the LORD has told you what is good, and this is what he requires of you: to do what is right, to love mercy, and to walk humbly with your God.

Matthew 23:23 (NLT)
"What sorrow awaits you teachers of religious law and you Pharisees. Hypocrites! For you are careful to tithe even the tiniest income from your herb gardens, but you ignore the more important aspects of the law-justice, mercy, and faith. You should tithe, yes, but do not neglect the more important things.

Mark 12:33 (NLT)
And I know it is important to love him with all my heart and all my understanding and all my strength, and to love my neighbor as myself. This is more important than to offer all of the burnt offerings and sacrifices required in the law."

NOTES:

SELF-HATRED & CONDEMNATION

A pattern of feeling deep disdain for oneself based on a conviction that we are somehow flawed at a core level.

Matthew 19:18–19 Jesus replied, "'Do not murder, do not commit adultery, do not steal, do not give false testimony, honor your father and mother,' and 'love your neighbor as yourself.'"

Thoughts on Self-Hatred and Condemnation

Matthew 5:21–22 You have heard that is was said to the people long ago, 'Do not murder,' and 'anyone who murders will be subject to judgment.' But I tell you that anyone who is angry with his brother will be subject to judgment…

The Amplified Bible translates the word "anger" in this passage as *resentment, hatred, enmity, or bitterness of heart*. Unfortunately, people often feel that way toward themselves.

The Second Great Commandment states that we are to love others as we love ourselves. In this command it is critical that we have a healthy regard and love for ourselves if we are to love others and have a healthy regard for others.

How we relate to ourselves will be projected in how we relate to others. If we are not healthy internally we will not be healthy externally and the best of circumstances cannot change that reality.

There are three primary relationships in which all of us must be healthy. The first is God, the second is others, and the third is ourselves. In Christian circles, we often think it is narcissism to concern ourselves with regard for ourselves.

But if we dislike ourselves, shame ourselves, and condemn ourselves, we are sinning against God and violating His Kingdom design for us. As we regard ourselves, so we act out and live our lives. Therefore, it is important for us to live with a healthy, God-given regard for ourselves. We must regard ourselves as God regards us.

Satan loves to get God's people mired in condemnation and self-hatred. When Christians are in that state, they will not only be ineffective for God and His Kingdom work, but they will totally miss the joy and fulfillment of living in the abundant life of God's design for them.

Biblical Examples

Most everyone has made decisions, choices, and committed acts and sins for which there is regret and sorrow. It is easy to get lost in the weeds of self-condemnation, self-hatred, and anger against yourself.

Yet, some have been violated, abused, and received injustices against them by others. It is easy in those situations to think you are the bad one, the dirty one, and of no intrinsic value.

In the Scriptures, the instances are many where people come before Jesus in condemnation and shame but leave His presence with life, hope, forgiveness, and a new perception of themselves. Whether it was Mary Magdalene, the woman at the well (John 4), the tax-collector (Luke 18:9), or the woman caught in adultery (John 8).

To be convicted of sin is a good thing. And with repentance there is immediate life and refreshment. Condemnation, on the other hand, leads to death.

Judas, after betraying Jesus, must have been consumed with self-condemnation and possible self-hatred for his acts of betraying Jesus. The result was that he committed suicide.

Peter also was consumed with remorse for his acts of betraying Jesus when Jesus needed him the most. But he received forgiveness and lived out an abundant life in God's purposes for him.

Characteristics of self-hatred and condemnation:

- ❑ feelings of inner anger, frustration, and disgust with myself
- ❑ feeling that something is wrong with me
- ❑ feeling as though I cannot forgive myself
- ❑ living with regret, shame, and guilt even though I have asked God's forgiveness and repented
- ❑ experiencing similar feelings (anger, frustration, disgust) toward others

RECOGNIZING SELF-HATRED AND CONDEMNATION

1. Self curses: Reliving of past and present mistakes

- ❏ I have trouble distinguishing myself from my sin; I allow my sin to define me as a person.
- ❏ I live with a low level of pain and sorrow because of things I have done in the past.
- ❏ When I make a mistake or a poor judgment call, my mind churns with thoughts like, "What an idiot!" "That was a stupid thing to say…" "I should have known better." I find it difficult to put it aside and move on.
- ❏ Because of mistakes I have made in the past, I find myself locked down when it comes to making decisions; I fear it will be the wrong decision and will hurt more than help.

2. Self-loathing: a negative filter that applies to everything I think about myself

- ❏ I am very uncomfortable being the center of attention, and will do almost anything to avoid it.
- ❏ When I look in the mirror, all I see is my flaws.
- ❏ I find it difficult to accept compliments. I disqualify and discount them in my head by saying, "They really don't mean it, because I know it's not true."
- ❏ I have difficulty seeing my gifts and strengths, and do not believe that others would be blessed by them.
- ❏ I often feel as though I am a burden to others. I will not ask for help because I feel I am bothering people.
- ❏ I am often silent in crowds because I feel like I am boring and do not make sense when I talk. At least people will think I am smart if I keep my mouth shut! I won't give myself away to others.

3. Self-blame: my present situation causes my to turn on myself

- ❏ I readily accept the blame for things with which I had nothing to do. I find myself apologizing often in conversations.
- ❏ After completing an assigned task or speaking out, I will beat myself up with all the things I wish I would have said. I replay situations over and over in my head. "Why did I say that?" "I failed to do what was asked of me," or "I could have done it better." Regret and shame reign uppermost in my thoughts.

- ❑ When someone unexpectedly wants to talk with me, I immediately suspect that I've done something wrong.
- ❑ I don't understand why people would want to spend time with me.

4. Denial: things I deny, defend, or hate about myself

- ❑ I am very hard on myself, and hold myself to high standards. I do this to others as well.
- ❑ I have a hard time forgiving myself and others. I quickly take offense for myself, or for others when I see them get hurt.
- ❑ I take everything said personally as criticism, rejection, or failing, even though it usually was not directed toward me.
- ❑ I have trouble seeing myself inside the circle and belonging. I see myself outside the circle, not wanted or needed. If I am invited in, I tend to resist until I am "persuaded" that others really want me.
- ❑ I find myself blaming others and wallowing in victimization and self-pity.
- ❑ I often look for hidden motives in what people say and do; I find it easy to think about things in a paranoid manner (for example, "What do they really mean or what are they really trying to say?").
- ❑ When I am around people, I find myself in a strange tension between wanting to hide in a corner while also desiring acceptance and recognition.

5. Self-destruction: hatred expressed inwardly or outwardly

- ❑ "Everyone would be better off and there wouldn't be any problems if I weren't here."
- ❑ If my sin is exposed, I feel as though I will disintegrate, so I have to keep it together. "I already hate what is inside me. "If they knew it, they would hate me too."
- ❑ It is too painful to look honestly at myself; I will focus on finding faults, blaming and criticizing, and not giving the benefit of the doubt to others instead.
- ❑ "Won't someone love me?" "I'll do anything to get attention." "If I can't get someone to love me, I might as well disappear."
- ❑ No one will accept me, so I'll reject them before they reject me.
- ❑ It is safer to withdraw into isolation than be around people. But once I'm with people, my brain goes around and around in endless negative self-talk, replaying conversations, and beating myself up. I end up defeated, confused, depressed, and angry at myself and others.
- ❑ I function in the rebellion of believing my emotions rather than believing God.
- ❑ I can believe God' promises for others, but not for me.
- ❑ Even though I know what I am doing to myself is not healthy, I still persist with eating disorders, addictions, sleep deprivation, _____(you fill in the blank). To tell the truth, I really don't care.

- ❏ When I read the Bible, I focus on God's warnings and judgment rather than on His grace, mercy, compassion, and love.

- ❏ When I think of God looking at me, I think He is frowning and frustrated with me.

- ❏ I find it difficult to believe He really has used, is using, or will use me in advancing His Kingdom here on Earth.

THE 4 Rs FOR SELF-HATRED AND CONDEMNATION

REPENTANCE

(Humbly submit yourself before God in repentance and receive forgiveness through Christ's death and resurrection.)

Sample Prayer: Heavenly Father, I ask Your forgiveness for my sin of hating what You love—namely, me! I ask Your forgiveness for not forgiving myself when You have forgiven me. Lord Jesus, I ask forgiveness for sinning against You, and saying in my heart that what You did on the cross for me was not enough and not embracing Your love for me. I ask forgiveness for comforting myself with the lies of darkness and death instead of running to You and allowing You to breathe Your life of love and light into my life. God, I confess my sin against You. I have grieved You by closing my ears to Your voice and running my life according to my emotions rather than trusting myself to Your wisdom and limitless power. (Specifically ask forgiveness for each box you checked, and any other sins that come to mind associated with each category.) I also ask forgiveness for the following ways self-hatred has played out in my life through my emotions and actions: _____. Now I turn in repentance, committing myself to breaking the patterns of self-hatred in my life.

REBUKE

(Resist the devil by rebuking him from any stronghold(s) in your life through the power of the death and resurrection of Jesus Christ. In God's authority, renounce any lies believed about God, yourself, or others.)

Sample Prayer: In the name of Jesus Christ, I rebuke every effort of the enemy to create a stronghold of self-hatred in my life. I rebuke every spirit that was given a foothold in my life due to the stronghold of self-hatred. I renounce the lie that I am unlovable.

REPLACE

(Replace self-hatred with a single-focused devotion to God and obedience. Ask God to renew your heart, mind, emotions and will through the empowering of the Holy Spirit.)

Sample Prayer: *Lord, renew my heart, mind, emotions and will through the truth of Your Word and empowering of Your Holy Spirit. I replace the "spirit of self-hatred" and all of its symptoms with Your Holy Spirit of power, love and discipline. Let the fruit of Your Spirit be evidenced in the relationships in my life by the following new behaviors (use list below):*

RECEIVE

(Request and receive the filling of the Holy Spirit for you to live supernaturally in God's forgiveness and regard for you.)

Sample Prayer: *Heavenly Father, I thank You for Your forgiveness, and I receive it fully. Lord, I ask that through the power of Your Spirit's work in me, grace and peace will be mine in abundance through my knowledge of You and of the Lord Jesus Christ. Your divine power has given me everything I need for life and godliness. I rejoice in the One who called me by His glory and goodness.*

WALKING IN THE OPPOSITE SPIRIT

- ❑ I will immerse myself in God's Word and learn the truth about His love for me.
- ❑ I will replace the feelings of self-loathing with joy in my identity as Christ's beloved.
- ❑ I will turn from every thought of self-condemnation and seek the face of God, who loves to be gracious to me.
- ❑ I will find joy in the ways God chooses to use me for His glory.
- ❑ I will seek to reach out to others with love and encouragement.
- ❑ I will give myself away in Kingdom ministry for the Lord's sake.
- ❑ I will see myself as one chosen of God, beloved in His sight, from this day forward.

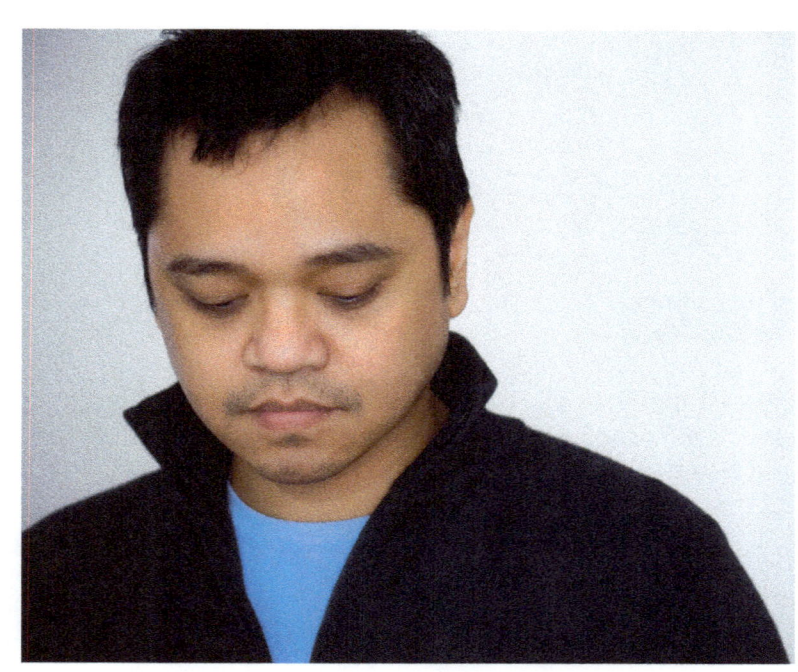

Practical Steps

Meditate on the scriptures listed below, inserting your name into each verse. Then, based on what you've learned, take some time to interact with the following questions:

1. How much love does God have?
2. How does God feel about me?
3. What God is doing for me right now?
4. What are God's promises for me in the future?
5. How is God describing me in His Word?
6. What is God instructing me to do?

SCRIPTURES:

John 3:16	**Psalm 138:1–18**	**Romans 8: 31–19**
Psalm 36:5–10	**1 John 4:7–21**	**1 Corinthians 13**
Psalm 37:18–40	**Ephesians 3:14–19**	
Psalm 42:8	**Colossians 3:12–17**	

Write out your answers, including the text of the appropriate verses.

SHAME

Shame is characterized by painful feelings of guilt and embarrassment for improper behavior, associated with acts committed by a person as well as against a person, usually carried in response to something hidden or kept secret. Related terms: disgrace; dishonor; deep feelings of embarrassment.

Shame causes us to withhold ourselves in all areas of life. In its shadow, we tend to form shallow and guarded relationships. We do not move boldly and confidently in the power and authority that is ours in Jesus Christ. Instead, we live in fear that someone will find out how dirty or inadequate we are (that is, that we think we are). Shame is like an unseen weight we drag through life.

Biblical Examples

We see shame first realized in Genesis 3. Adam and Eve had just violated and betrayed God in their sin of independence and rebellion. One of the first recognized consequences of their sin was "shame." It affected their relationships with each other and God. We read in Genesis 2:25; 3:7 (NLT):

Now the man and his wife were both naked, but they felt no shame. . . . At that moment [after their sin] their eyes were opened, and they suddenly felt shame at their nakedness. So they sewed fig leaves together to cover themselves. When the cool evening breezes were blowing, the man and his wife heard the Lord God walking about in the garden. So they hid from the Lord God among the trees. Then the Lord God called to the man, "Where are you?" He replied, "I heard you walking in the garden, so I hid. I was afraid because I was naked."

The story of the "prodigal son" (Luke 15:11–32) demonstrates how sin leads to a quagmire of shame. It also shows the father's generous and outlandish response of grace and love to the returning son (Jesus' purpose in the story). He returns the son to a place honor and position.

God's Design

You may have, or currently live with some shame in your life. Shame is not God's plan for how His children should live. His Word tells us, "No one whose hope is in you will ever be put to shame" (Psalm 25:3, NIV). He wants us to bring our burdens of shame to Him and allow Him to lift them. But as long as our sins and our shame remain in the dark, they are a part of Satan's kingdom. He has jurisdiction over them—a legal right. When we confess our sins and bring them out into the light beforeGod, we break the hold Satan has over them. God forgives. God cleanses. God restores. God makes us righteous with His righteousness. We are free!

> 1 John 1:9 (NIV) *If we confess our sins, he is faithful and just and will forgive us our sins and purify us from all unrighteousness.*
>
> Isaiah 61:10 (NIV) *I delight greatly in the Lord; my soul rejoices in my God. For he has clothed me with garments of salvation and arrayed me in a robe of righteousness, as a bridegroom adorns his head like a priest, and as a bride adorns herself with her jewels.*

Hopelessness is often related to shame. Hopelessness makes us feel the pain, sorrow, discouragement, and condemnation we are feeling will never be lifted. We give up hoping for joy, peace, and happiness. We give up hoping for real, lasting freedom. This too is a lie of the enemy.

DIAGNOSTIC QUESTIONS:

The following diagnostic questions will help you identify if and how you are living out of or with shame. Please check any boxes that resonate with you:

My Relationships with God and Others

- ❑ I do not feel I can be forgiven for this sin.
- ❑ It is hard for me to believe that God can forgive even this.
- ❑ I cannot tell anyone about this, including God, because it is so shameful.
- ❑ I can't believe God finds any pleasure in me.
- ❑ I am afraid others might know about my sin.
- ❑ I have trouble forming trusting relationships because I guard against getting too "vulnerable" with others.
- ❑ I am very fearful that others can discern my ugly sin; this causes me to fear drawing close to anyone, including God.

- ❏ I live in constant fear of how others will regard me if my past or present sin is known.
- ❏ I hate for others to see me blow it.
- ❏ When someone points a sin out to me, I want to run and hide because I am so embarrassed.
- ❏ People think they know me, but no one really does.
- ❏ I am afraid in small groups that someone will ask about my personal life.

Self-Condemnation

- ❏ I tend to think negatively about myself, and I battle negative thoughts about myself continuously.
- ❏ I beat myself up regarding my sin and weakness toward sin.
- ❏ I try to offset these condemning thoughts by pushing myself to succeed in other areas (work, school, athletics, etc).
- ❏ I feel dirty, ruined, or like "damaged goods."
- ❏ I have trouble finding intimacy with God.
- ❏ I seem unable to forgive myself.
- ❏ I feel that I could never marry a godly man/woman because he/she might find out about my sin and reject me.
- ❏ I don't believe I can lead others; my sin has made me unworthy.

My Mindset and Thinking

- ❏ I cannot stop thinking about this!
- ❏ I regularly deal with disturbing memories of my shameful experience(s).
- ❏ I have disturbing dreams and visions about my sin.
- ❏ Given my past, I can't believe I'll ever feel completely "clean."
- ❏ I will never be able to have deep relationships with others because I must make sure they never learn the truth about this sin.
- ❏ I am "damaged goods."
- ❏ I am unworthy.
- ❏ I tend to think negatively about myself, battling these thoughts continuously.

- ❏ I often wish I could just be someone else instead of who I am.
- ❏ It's hard for me to imagine that God sees anything good in me.
- ❏ I often feel as if God is angry with me, even when I haven't specifically sinned.
- ❏ Some things in my life are too shameful to talk about with anyone.
- ❏ I live with a feeling that there is something inherently wrong with me.
- ❏ I feel I don't deserve a joyful life in Christ.
- ❏ I find it easier to pretend everything is fine than to share with others when I am struggling in my spiritual walk.

THE INJUSTICE OF SHAME:

Often we take on an identity of shame, and we do things that bring shame on ourselves because acts or words of shame were imposed on us by others. Take time identify any persons, situations, and words that caused you shame.

Person(s) or Situation(s)	Actions/Words toward You	How It Wounded You

GRANT FORGIVENESS

In prayer, you need to give forgiveness (personally forgive) to each person/situation, for what they did and said to you, and specifically for what it did to you. Be thorough!

THE 4 Rs FOR SHAME

REPENTANCE

Shame causes us to respond to life and God's truth in sinful ways in many different areas. It is important to identify each one and confess the sins related to it. Apply the following prayer to your situation.

Sample Prayer: *Lord Jesus, I ask for Your forgiveness for this sin of carrying shame. I repent of all the ways I have allowed them to be a part of my life. I see how they have affected me and others around me. I name it as sin. Shame is not from You!* (Go back through the boxes you checked and ask God to forgive you in each area.)

REBUKE

Renounce every lie that you have held onto concerning your person or your behavior. In the authority of Jesus Christ, rebuke/resist Satan and any evil spirits that have found a place to oppress you through shameful thoughts and feelings and close the door firmly on their activity in your life. The following prayer is suggested for taking authority over your sin and the enemy who works against you.

Sample Prayer: *Lord, I renounce the life and ways of shame. That is not who I am, and it does not represent You. I rebuke every evil spirit of shame for attacking me with thoughts of shame, disgrace, and unworthiness. I come against you by the authority of Jesus Christ, and I command you to flee right now. You are liars, and I will no longer listen to you and your deceptions about me. According to the Word of God, I put them under my feet, and I crush the influence they have had in my life.*

REPLACE

Acknowledge and affirm that God has created you. Use the Scriptures above, or others, claim that you will no longer hide your shame, but will walk in the light as He is in the light.

Sample Prayer: *I replace the life of shame with acceptance and recognition of being truly and fully a child of God. I replace shame by living a life of joy, peace, courage, boldness, strength, authority, and love that will give a reason for the world to ask me about the reason for the hope* *in my life. I will live in the truth of courage, boldness, and confidence that rightfully belongs to those who are children of God.*

RECEIVE

Ask the Holy Spirit to fill you with the God's life in every place that shame once inhabited you. Thank the Lord that He has forgiven your every sin and has cleansed you from all unrighteousness, even the effects of other people's sins against you. Receive His full cleansing and rejoice. The following prayer is a suggested model for you, but however you pray, pray from your heart.

Sample Prayer: *Lord Jesus, I now ask for and receive in faith the infilling of Your Holy Spirit that I might live a God-empowered life that lives above all shame. I walk in the hope, confidence, power, and authority that are mine as the child of the King of kings. I am accepted, and a living testimony of God's love, grace, and glory!*

WALKING IN THE OPPOSITE SPIRIT

Shame can be insidious, hidden in your thought life in dozens of ways of which you may not be aware. It is critical that you immerse yourself in the truth of God's Word about who you are in Christ, and make a choice every day to believe what He has said, resisting the lies of the evil one who wants to draw you back into shame.

Part of living free in Christ and walking in real purity and holiness depends on having our minds renewed by God's Word and His Holy Spirit. Use the truth of God's Word and the authority you have in Christ to fight and renounce the lies of the enemy when they come back to torment your thoughts.

Meditation on the promises of God about God's forgiveness is essential. Meditating on God's truth will cut down the lies that accuse you of being "unclean," and will be a source of comfort as well as a reminder of your true standing before the Lord. Do not allow old mental videos, the words of others, and thoughts of worthlessness or guilt to define you. Those are not who you are!

Shame masquerades itself as false humility. There is nothing humble about not trusting in the finished work of Christ on the cross. Because He died for you, you are free from shame, no matter what is in your past.

- I will never be put to shame because I put my trust in Him. (Romans 9:33)
- I will never be put to shame because my hope is in Him. (Psalm 25:3)
- I will humble myself and pray, and He will forgive my sin and heal me. (2 Chronicles 7:14)
- I look to Him, and I am radiant; my face is never covered with shame. (Psalm 34:5)
- I have been given a new heart, and a new spirit has been put in me. (Ezekiel 36:26)
- I am in Christ Jesus; therefore there is no condemnation! (Romans 8:1)
- I will never again be ashamed, for God has worked wonders for me. (Joel 2:26)
- I am God's workmanship, created in Christ Jesus to do good works. (Ephesians 2:10)

- I am redeemed and forgiven of all my sins! (Colossians 1:14)
- I will believe that I have been given the very righteousness of Christ. (2 Corinthians 5:21)

Scriptures

> **SCRIPTURES:**
>
> **Psalm 25:3**
> *Indeed, none of those who wait for you will be ashamed. . . .*
>
> **Romans 8:1**
> *Therefore there is now no condemnation for those who are in Christ Jesus.*
>
> **Psalm 34:5**
> *They looked to Him and were radiant, and their faces will never be ashamed.*
>
> **1 Corinthians 5:17**
> *Therefore if anyone is in Christ, he is a new creature; the old things passed away; behold, the new things have come.*
>
> **Revelation 21:5**
> *And He who sits on the throne said, "Behold, I am making all things new" and He said, "Write, for these words are faithful and true."*

NOTES:

UNBELIEF

Unbelief is distrust in God's word, character, and person. It is the antithesis to faith and trust. Unbelief is a determined refusal to believe and trust which results in disobedience and rebellion toward God.

Unbelief seems harmless enough to most Christians. It's just an innocent flaw—isn't it? We consider it more a matter of practicality, caution, or prudence. In fact, unbelief fearfully, stubbornly, or rebelliously doubts the Word, the work, and the character of God, and it expresses those doubts in both word and action. It asserts that we have a better gauge on reality than He does. It gives preeminence to our assumptions, presuppositions, prejudices, and fears.

Consider some of the characteristics of unbelief:

- Makes up its mind about what God can and can't do, what He will or won't do, and how He does or doesn't operate

- It finds its methods for accomplishing God's business, both personally and corporately

- It looks inward instead of upward. As Jim Cymbala writes in *Fresh Faith*, "Unbelief talks to itself instead of talking to God."

Rather than seeking the Lord and acting in faith according to His character and truth, we depend on our understanding, our methods, and our strength for life and ministry. This tendency toward unbelief often is rooted in fear, pride, rebellion, or other sin areas:

- When motivated by fear, unbelief may manifest itself in self-protective coping mechanisms, like those encountered when dealing with insecurity and inferiority.

- When stemming from pride or rebellion, unbelief masks itself as realism, intellectualism, or practicality.

- In the church, unbelief cloaks itself in a critical, religious spirit, as in the case of the Pharisees in Jesus' day.

BIBLICAL EXAMPLE

One glaring biblical example is the account when Israel, in their unbelief, failed to trust God and enter the Promised Land.

> Deuteronomy 1:32–35 (ESV) *Yet in spite of this word you did not believe the LORD your God, who went before you in the way to seek you out a place to pitch your tents, in fire by night and in the cloud by day, to show you by what way you should go. "And the LORD heard your words and was angered, and he swore, 'Not one of these men of this evil generation shall see the good land that I swore to give to your fathers,*

The full version of this account is found in Numbers 13:1–14:38. The report in Deuteronomy is a sobering account of the seriousness and consequences of unbelief. Following their miraculous deliverance from slavery in Egypt, the Israelites were approaching the much-anticipated Promised Land. Instead of entering boldly in faith, they panicked. Deuteronomy 1:22 tells us that it was the people who initiated the idea of spying out the land.

What they saw both awed and frightened them. It stirred up doubt and insecurity. It caused division and rebellion. Thus, they brought ruin on themselves by trusting in what they could see and understand with their natural senses, rather than in God's divine revelation. Only Joshua and Caleb brought back a good report. They saw the same things as the other spies with their physical eyes, but they saw things differently with their spiritual eyes. They looked at the land through the lens of God's promises, His faithfulness, and His power. They perceived not in fear but in faith.

The people, however, gave more credit to the report of the practical-sounding spies than to the word of God. So, they missed out on the blessings of the Promised Land and spent the remainder of their days wandering in a desolate wilderness for their unbelief.

Even though it may be deeply hidden, unbelief never goes unseen or unnoticed. The Scriptures make it clear that God counts unbelief as a grave sin, and He deals with it forcefully. Faith renders nothing impossible with God, and has the potential to move mountains, Jesus said. Without it, as we are reminded in Hebrews 11:6, it is impossible to please God.

FRUITS OF UNBELIEF

- obstructs God's presence and power in our lives
- opens the door to taking offense, especially toward God and many times toward those who are living in obedience to God
- nurtures a root of skepticism
- hinders prayer
- leads to instability
- feeds a critical attitude
- desensitizes God's people to the Holy Spirit and to spiritual things
- poisons others
- fosters arrogance and pride
- undercuts people's regard for God's Word and His character
- holds up my own standard as the correct standard, even placing it ahead of the Lord's standard
- brings discouragement to others and dampens their faith
- incurs God's disappointment, anger, and disfavor
- hinders the release and the activity of the Holy Spirit
- leads to control

RECOGNIZING UNBELIEF

Ask the Holy Spirit to examine your heart as you consider the following checklist. Check all that apply:

- ❑ I find myself being disappointed—even offended—that God doesn't seem to work as I believe He should, or answer my prayers in the way I'd like.
- ❑ When I hear of others' experiences of God's presence, power, or answered prayer, I am skeptical. My usual first reaction is to try to analyze or disprove their claim.
- ❑ I try to pass off a critical spirit as being a Berean spirit ("spiritually discerning" and "protecting"—see Acts 17:11).
- ❑ I am critical of the direction and methods of church and ministry leaders.
- ❑ I tend to be suspicious of others.

- ❑ I wonder why the Holy Spirit doesn't seem to talk to me or use me as powerfully as He uses others.
- ❑ I doubt that God really speaks to or uses others as they claim because I don't see Him speaking to me or using me in those ways.
- ❑ I tend to be self-sufficient and independent from others; if I'm honest about it, I tend to be self-sufficient and independent from God.
- ❑ I first perceive people and situations as impossible, rather than possible with God.
- ❑ I am not confident that I have spiritual authority through Jesus Christ.
- ❑ I am not motivated to pray consistently, and I have little interest in intercessory or spiritual warfare prayer.
- ❑ Prayer is usually a last resort for me. I try to figure things out or work them out for myself first. My actions would indicate I believe that God helps those who help themselves.
- ❑ I succumb to habitual behaviors and addictions (coping mechanisms) to comfort me when I feel discouraged, afraid, hopeless, hurt, etc.
- ❑ I make decisions based on my fears rather than on what I know God wants me to do in a given situation (where to go, how to get there, what my spouse/children can do, or where they can go, etc.).
- ❑ I think my situation, my sins, my fears, my marriage, my spiritual life, my (you fill in the blank) will never change.
- ❑ I panic when I receive bad or distressing news, or even the suggestion that something bad or distressing may occur.

- ❑ I tend to be worried, fearful, and anxious about many things.
- ❑ I fear that my children or other family members will never be saved.
- ❑ I try to control people, situations, and even God, because I am afraid to let go and trust Him to care for them, to lead them, to protect them, to save them, etc.
- ❑ I am skeptical of the present-day supernatural work of the Holy Spirit.
- ❑ I fear taking the risk of praying and ministering boldly with others in areas like healing or spiritual freedom.
- ❑ I fear stepping out in faith in response to confirmed revelation God has given to me or to others in the body of Christ.
- ❑ Visible circumstances have a stronger influence on me than do the written Word, spoken words, or the character of God.

WALKING IN THE OPPOSITE SPIRIT

Realize that behind every fear and unbelief lurks a lie. The problem is the lie that we believe about God's perceived inability to protect, provide, comfort, strengthen, and equip us for every circumstance in life.

- ❏ You must make the decision to hate the sin of unbelief with a holy violence. It grieves God's heart, for it denies the reality of His awesome provision and protection.
- ❏ Confess all specific areas of unbelief.
- ❏ Ask God to reveal any areas and root issues that are still unknown to you. Consider asking someone to pray with you about this. They may have insight or receive Holy Spirit revelation about areas of unbelief that are blind spots to you.
- ❏ Renounce unbelief in the name of Jesus and rebuke the enemy by the name of Jesus. Firmly command the enemy to go and stand in faith (use the 4Rs).

Then move "in the opposite spirit"—in the opposite direction—of your unbelief. It is not enough to only confess; now you must face your areas of unbelief aggressively, receive God's love and promises, and replace all unbelief with confident affirmation of the truth of God's Word and character.

THE 4 Rs FOR UNBELIEF

REPENTANCE

Take responsibility for unbelief by confessing specifically your own sinful rejection of God's character and Word. Name areas of unbelief specifically—finances, relationships, spiritual life, etc.

Sample Prayer: Father, I confess that I Have chosen to trust in my own strength, wisdom, and abilities because I doubted You would meet all my needs. I confess that I have not believed Your Word to be true, and I have not trusted that You are perfect in all Your ways. I confess unbelief in the areas of_____ (name these) and ask You to forgive me and cleanse me from all unrighteousness.

REBUKE

Renounce every lie you have bought into that reflects a stubborn heart of unbelief. Renounce lies about God's character and lies about His promises to provide. Sever all association with the evil of unbelief by the power of Christ in you. In the authority of Jesus Christ, resist Satan and any evil spirits that have found a place to oppress you through your sin of unbelief and close the door firmly on their activity in your life.

> **Sample Prayer:** *I renounce the lie that God is not sufficient for me emotionally, physically, financially, mentally, relationally, and spiritually. I renounce the lie that God does not care for me nor look out for my best interests. I sever every association I have had with a doubting spirit by the blood of Jesus Christ. In His Name I rebuke and resist every spirit of unbelief, evil, scorn, doubt, skepticism, and fear. You no longer have access to my life though unbelief, so I command you to flee now.*

REPLACE

Acknowledge and embrace the truth about God's sovereign power, love, and perfect wisdom. Speak out declarations demonstrate that you now want to live in the spirit of faith and trust instead of unbelief.

> **Sample Prayer:** *I declare I will live a life of faith that is placed in the Word, character, love, and power of God. I will exercise my faith and grow in my faith, most importantly when the circumstances around me could be a source of unbelief and fear. The areas I specifically will walk in faith are _____ (name these specifically).*

RECEIVE

Thank the Lord for how He has freely forgiven you. Receive his full cleansing and rejoice. Ask Him to fill every place that was once inhabited by the sin of unbelief with the fullness of the Holy Spirit. In faith receive the filling of the Holy Spirit to live your supernatural life.

> **Sample Prayer:** *I request and receive the filling of Your Spirit into my life right now to live the supernatural life of faith in You and Your truth. Lord, thank you for forgiving and cleansing me completely. I receive Your full forgiveness.*

LIVING FREE OF UNBELIEF

As we grow in our willingness and ability to live in freedom, we are challenged to face areas in which we may have little or no previous experience. We look at our physical, psychological, and emotional resources and realize they are inadequate or the demands of life, ministry, and spiritual battle. We begin to see the enormous gap between what we can do in our strength (natural) and what we can do in the power of the Holy Spirit (supernatural).

That gap is bridged when we look not at our own hands and our inadequacies, but when we step out in faith to do what Jesus said we would do, should do, and could do! Every time we take these steps of faith and something supernatural happens, our faith—and our confidence—is reinforced. Faith diminishes fear just as fear diminishes faith!

Believing God requires both faith and trust. Faith knows that God is willing and able to fulfill what He says He will do. Trust is placing yourself squarely in line with that knowledge and committing yourself to walk in it even before you see it happen with your natural eyes. Faith knows that God's hands can sustain and secure you. Trust jumps into those hands.

Faith and trust are two distinct but interlocking components of believing God. But it's hard to trust what you don't know. That's why Scripture says that faith comes by hearing the Word of God (Romans 10:17). It's much easier to trust something or someone that you know intimately. Do you know God's Word? Do you know His promises, His character, and His power?

Make the following affirmations:

- I will renounce fear and unbelief and replace them with faith and confidence in the Word, the character, and the power of God.

- I will not live only by what I see and understand with my natural senses or with my emotional reactions, but according to the Scriptures and revealed promises of God.

- I will always seek to honor Him, and I will not dishonor Him or those who are seeking to walk in obedience and in large faith.

- I will ask the Lord daily to increase my faith.

- I will spend more time in the Word, so I can know God's work, character, and promises more fully.

- I will learn to hear His voice and to act on it.

- I will not live in rebellion by fearing the natural consequences of obedience to God.

- I will not hide an unbelieving, critical spirit under the guise of being practical, prudent, or "Berean."

- I will wait for God to fulfill His promises; I will not rely on my own schemes, false comforts, coping mechanisms, or control.

- I will step out boldly in faith to minister in ways that Jesus did.

- I will live and minister confidently in the spiritual authority that is mine through Jesus Christ.

- I will live above my emotions and circumstances, trusting fully in God to provide for, to protect, and to empower me.

- I will not fear or rebel against the supernatural work of the Holy Spirit.

- I will cultivate a culture of faith with those around me, beginning with my family, and including my ministry, my church family, and my friends.

SCRIPTURES:

Psalm 78:19–22
They spoke against God, saying, "Can God spread a table in the desert? When he struck the rock, water gushed out, and streams flowed abundantly. But can he also give us food? Can he supply meat for his people?" When the LORD heard them, he was very angry; his fire broke out against Jacob, and his wrath rose against Israel, for they did not believe in God or trust in his deliverance.

Matthew 6:25–30 (NIV)
That is why I tell you not to worry about everyday life—whether you have enough food and drink, or enough clothes to wear. Isn't life more than food, and your body more than clothing? Look at the birds. They don't plant or harvest or store food in barns, for your heavenly Father feeds them. And aren't you far more valuable to him than they are? Can all your worries add a single moment to your life? And why worry about your clothing? Look at the lilies of the field and how they grow. They don't work or make their clothing, yet Solomon in all his glory was not dressed as beautifully as they are. And if God cares so wonderfully for wildflowers that are here today and thrown into the fire tomorrow, he will certainly care for you. Why do you have so little faith?

Matthew 13:58
And he did not do many miracles there because of their lack of faith.

Hebrews 11:1
Now faith is being sure of what we hope for and certain of what we do not see.

Hebrews 11:6
And without faith it is impossible to please God, because anyone who comes to him must believe that he exists and that he rewards those who earnestly seek him.

NOTES:

UNFORGIVENESS

An unwillingness (intentional or unintentional) to release someone from offending or sinning against you.

"And be kind to one another, tenderhearted, forgiving each other, just as God in Christ also has forgiven you." Ephesians 4:32 NASB

One of the most potent weapons of the enemy against humanity is unforgiveness. It produces fruits of bitterness, anger, and rage, and can even lead to murder. It also gives great jurisdiction to the enemy in our lives. Unforgiveness lays the foundation for destructive behavioral patterns.

The contrast of unforgiveness is "forgiveness." Forgiveness is the very foundation of God's Kingdom and the very nature of God Himself. Loosed from the bondage that unforgiveness brings, we can begin to heal, and the real love of God can begin to flow out of our lives towards others.

Joseph Models Forgiveness

Joseph's life is a classic example of the power of forgiveness—and unforgiveness. The story begins with the birth of Joseph, son of Jacob by his wife, Rachel. Joseph was the youngest of 11 brothers, and he was his father's favorite "because he was the son of his old age" (Genesis 37:3).

Unfortunately for Joseph, his father Jacob did not conceal the fact that Joseph was his favorite. Jacob made a beautiful coat of honor for Joseph, something usually given only to the firstborn son. When Jacob presented that particular garment to Joseph, his half-brothers began to hate him.

Joseph also had dreams. In his youthful indiscretion and pride, he readily shared the dreams with his brothers, relating how they would be subordinate to him. Jealousy and hatred filled Joseph's brothers' hearts. This unforgiveness caused the brothers to dream of ways to harm Joseph, even kill him.

One day Jacob sent Joseph with provisions for the brothers working out in the fields. Resentment and bitterness had had several years to brew and were about to produce their evil fruit. (Genesis 37).

Joseph arrived in their camp with provisions from home. Joseph's brothers threw him into the pit to die, but his brother Reuben pleaded with them to spare Joseph's life. A band of Ishmaelite traders passed by on their way to Egypt. Joseph's brothers sold him to the traders for 20 pieces of silver.

Joseph was sold on the slave block to Potiphar (Pharaoh's chief officer) as a house slave. Joseph found favor with Potiphar. Potiphar's wife made an overt sexual advance on Joseph from which he fled. However, she unjustly accused Joseph of rape, so he was thrown into prison even though he was innocent.

If anyone had reasons for unforgiveness, it was Joseph. He had every "right" to become bitter and angry, filled with rage, self-pity, resentment, and all the rest.

Joseph may have been in prison, but he was not in the self-imposed prison of unforgiveness! He eventually was miraculously released from prison and became the second in command over all of Egypt under Pharaoh. A severe famine followed. Jacob sent Joseph's brothers to Egypt to seek provisions and they found themselves in front of Joseph, asking for food. They did not recognize Joseph, but he did them, and provided them with a great dinner and treated them kindly—not once, but twice. When he could take it no longer, he revealed his identity.

> *Then Joseph said to his brothers, "Please come closer to me." And they came closer. And he said, "I am your brother Joseph, whom you sold into Egypt. Now do not be grieved or angry with yourselves, because you sold me here, for God sent me before you to preserve life. For the famine has been in the land these two years, and there are still five years in which there will be neither plowing nor harvesting. God sent me before you to preserve for you a remnant in the earth, and to keep you alive by a great deliverance. Now, therefore, it was not you who sent me here, but God; and He has made me a father to Pharaoh and lord of all his household and ruler over all the land of Egypt."* Genesis 45:1–8

Joseph forgave, a stark contrast to the brothers' regard for Joseph when he was younger.

The key to forgiveness: releasing a debt

Forgiveness is necessary when we have been violated in one way or another. There is a debt to pay before reconciliation or restoration can take place. The debt might be emotional, relational, financial, or physical; the debt might be the result of a betrayal, or injustice. Regardless of the situation, a debt is owed to us.

To forgive, we must determine that we will release the offender from their debt to us. We will not expect the offender to settle the debt. Forgiving a debt out of mercy is what Jesus did when He released us from having to pay the liability for the sins and violations we committed against Him.

Common misunderstandings about forgiveness:

1. Pretending it did not happen
2. You must feel affection for the offender (you don't have to become best friends)

DIAGNOSING UNFORGIVENESS

- ❑ I find myself holding grudges.
- ❑ I retreat into isolation from others.
- ❑ I erupt in anger, or I boil inside.
- ❑ I think of ways to get even with others who have hurt me.
- ❑ I "just bury" the wrongs done to me without really addressing them.
- ❑ I pity myself.
- ❑ I carry bitterness and anger against those who have offended me or willfully wronged me.
- ❑ Instead of stating the truth, I make excuses for those who have hurt or wronged me.
- ❑ I often feel sorry for myself.
- ❑ Occasionally I think I'm some kind of a martyr.
- ❑ "Nobody has had it as bad as me."
- ❑ I want to get even with people who have caused me pain.
- ❑ I insulate and protect myself behind a wall of defensiveness.
- ❑ I do not trust others.
- ❑ I just "can't" forgive (usually means I won't forgive).
- ❑ I am angry with God for allowing "bad things" to happen to me.

- ❏ I act "like nothing happened" instead of addressing issues that have hurt me.
- ❏ I "can't get over" my past.

Forgiveness on Three Levels

When we forgive it is critical that we forgive on three levels:

1. the person(s) or group who harmed or violated you
2. what they did to harm or violate you
3. what the harm or violation did to you (make you feel and the consequences)

It is important that you are specific and thorough. This format is to provide you with a structured example to help you get started in the process of forgiving those who have sinned against you.

Person A (Name)	
What they did (incident 1)	What they did (incident 2)
Emotional & Practical Consequences	Emotional & Practical Consequences
Person B (Name)	
What they did (incident 1)	What they did (incident 2)
Emotional & Practical Consequences	Emotional & Practical Consequences

THE 4 Rs FOR UNFORGIVENESS

REPENTANCE

After you have forgiven those who have sinned against you, take responsibility for your unforgiveness and specifically confess the sin of unforgiveness.

There are often other sins that accompany unforgiveness such as anger, pride, bitterness, and resentment. Confess and ask forgiveness for those sins as well.

Sample Prayer: *Lord, I forgive the persons (name them), what they did to me (identify the actions and events) and what it has done to me (name the specific emotional, spiritual, physical, and practical consequences).*

I repent of the sin of unforgiveness. I call it out as sin and along with anger, resentment, and bitterness.

REBUKE

Renounce every lie you have held onto concerning your unforgiveness of people and situations in your life. In the authority of Jesus Christ, resist Satan and any evil spirits that have found a place to empower unforgiveness in you.

Sample Prayer: *I rebuke and bind the lies of the enemy right now. Their attack on my life in the area of unforgiveness is broken. I sever all ties to the stronghold of unforgiveness. I rebuke every evil spirit that has empowered unforgiveness in me. I command you to the feet of Jesus to receive His judgment for you.*

REPLACE

It takes an absolute hatred for the sin of unforgiveness in order to walk free of it. It is a deep cleansing of part of your personality, including your ways of thinking, your reactions, and your motives. When you begin to feel internal angst, bitterness, anger, or resentment; you must forgive and bless until it is done with conviction and it hurts no more.

Sample Prayer: *I right now declare by God's grace that I will live in forgiveness and mercy toward those who have hurt and wounded me. I trust God with my well-being and I entrust these individuals who have hurt me and to the Lord for Him to deal with on my behalf.*

RECEIVE

Request and receive the filling of the Holy Spirit to fill every place that was once inhabited by the sin of unforgiveness. Thank the Lord that He has totally forgiven you. Receive His full cleansing and rejoice.

Sample Prayer: *Lord, fill me with Your Holy Spirit that I may live supernaturally in the freedom of faith and trust in You and to serve others. I receive Your forgiveness for the sin of unforgiveness in my life.*

WALKING IN THE OPPOSITE SPIRIT

- ❏ I will forgive others just like God has forgiven me.
- ❏ I will choose to confront issues, to offer forgiveness to the perpetrator(s), and leave the rest to God.
- ❏ I will grow more and more in understanding that the hurts of my past never escaped the eyes of the Lord.
- ❏ I will not let Satan keep me in the bondage of unforgiveness.
- ❏ I will forgive others *regardless* of their response to me.
- ❏ I will allow others to see God's grace, mercy, and forgiveness at work in me.
- ❏ I will know and understand that forgiveness brings freedom and release from my past and present hurts.

SCRIPTURES:

Psalm 25:7
Forgive the rebellious sins of my youth; look instead through the eyes of your unfailing love, for you are merciful, O Lord.

Psalm 25:11
For the honor of your name, O Lord, forgive my many, many sins.

Psalm 130:4
But you offer forgiveness, that we might learn to fear you.

Matthew 18:21–35
Then Peter came to Him and asked, "Lord, how often should I forgive someone who sins against me? Seven times?" "No!" Jesus replied. "Seventy times seven!

Mark 11:25–26
And when you stand praying, if you hold anything against anyone, forgive him, so that your Father in heaven may forgive you your sins."

Ephesians 4:32
Be kind and compassionate to one another, forgiving each other, just as in Christ God forgave you.

Colossians 3:13
You must make allowance for each other's faults and forgive the person who offends you. Remember, the Lord forgave you, so you must forgive others.

James 2:13
For there will be no mercy for you if you have not been merciful to others. But if you have been merciful, then God's mercy toward you will win out over his judgment against you.

A TESTIMONY

Corrie Ten Boom and her beloved sister were prisoners in Ravensbruck, where they saw and were subjected to the atrocities of the Holocaust. The following episode occurred within months after the end of World War II and Corrie's release from the concentration camp. It's a gutsy account of forgiveness!

It was in a church in Munich that I saw him—a balding, heavy-set man in a gray overcoat, a brown felt hat clutched between his hands. People were filing out of the basement room where I had just spoken, moving along the rows of wooden chairs to the door at the rear. It was 1947 and I had come from Holland to defeated Germany with the message that God forgives.

The solemn faces stared back at me, not quite daring to believe. There were never questions after a talk in Germany in 1947. People stood up in silence, in silence collected their wraps, in silence left the room.

And that's when I saw him working his way forward against the others. One moment I saw the overcoat and the brown hat; the next, a blue uniform and a visored cap with its skull and crossbones. It came back with a rush: that huge room with its hard, overhead lights; the pathetic pile of dresses and shoes in the center of the floor; the shame of walking naked past this man. I could see my sister's frail form ahead of me, ribs sharp beneath the parchment of skin. Betsie, how thin you were!

The place was Ravensbruck and the man who was making his way forward had been a guard—one of the cruelest guards; I would recognize him anywhere.

Now he was in front of me, hand thrust out: "A fine message, Fraulein! How good it is to know that, as you say, all our sins are at the bottom of the sea!"

Now I, who had spoken so glibly of forgiveness, fumbled in my pocketbook rather than take that hand. He could not remember me of course—how could he remember one prisoner among those thousands of women? But I remembered him and the leather crop swinging from his belt. I was face to face with one of my captors and my blood seemed to freeze.

"You mentioned Ravensbruck in your talk," he was saying. "I was a guard there." No, he did not remember me.

"But since that time, I became a Christian. I know that God has forgiven me for the cruel things I did there, but I would like to hear it from you lips as well. Fraulein"—again the hand came out—"will you forgive me?"

I stood there—I whose sins had again and again needed to be forgiven—and I could not forgive. Betsie had died in that place - could he erase her slow, terrible death simply for the asking?

It could not have been many seconds that he stood there—hand held out—but to me it seemed hours as I wrestled with the most difficult thing I had ever had to do.

For I had to do it - I knew that. The message was that God forgives those who have injured us. I knew it not only as a commandment of God, but as a daily experience.

Since the end of the war I had a home in Holland for the victims of Nazi brutality. Those who were able to forgive their former enemies were able also to return to the outside world and rebuild their lives, no matter what the physical scars. Those who nursed their bitterness remained invalids. It was as simple and as horrible as that.

And still I stood there with the coldness clutching my heart. But forgiveness is not an emotion—I knew that too. Forgiveness is an act of the will, and the will can function regardless of the temperature of the heart. "Jesus, help me!" I prayed silently. "I can lift my hand. I can do that much. You supply the feeling."

And so woodenly, mechanically, I thrust my hand into the one stretched out to me. And as I did, an incredible thing took place. The current started in my shoulder, raced down my arm and sprang into our joined hands. And then this healing warmth seemed to flood my whole being, bringing tears to my eyes.

"I forgive you, brother!" I cried. "With all my heart."

For a moment we grasped each other's hands—the former guard and the former prisoner. I had never known God's love so intensely as I did then. But even so, I realized it was not my love. I had tried and did not have the power. It was the power of the Holy Spirit transforming me in God's love.

NOTES:

ABOUT THE AUTHOR

Dr. Michael (Mike) D. Riches, D. Min., has served as a lead pastor for over 40 years, and is currently in full-time pastoral ministry, along with his wife, Cindy, in Gig Harbor, Washington, where he serves as lead pastor of Harborview Fellowship.

Since 2001, Mike has ministered around the United States and overseas as the Founder and Director of The Sycamore Commission (www.sycamorecommission.org), a growing international teaching and equipping ministry committed to the support and reformation of the Church. Believing strongly that Jesus intended for His mission to continue with His disciples both then and now, the focus of the Sycamore Commission's ministry is to serve the Body of Christ by helping church leaders, churches, and individual Christians understand, fully recover, and live out the powerful, life-changing, Kingdom-advancing ministry of Jesus Christ.

Mike's ministry involves teaching, training, leadership development and support, and freedom prayer training. He has authored *Living Free: Recovering God's Design for Your Life, Living Set Free in Christ, Foundations of Freedom, Hearing God's Voice for Yourself and Others* (co-authored with Tom Jonez) and the *Freedom Prayer Training* course.

Also from Sycamore Publications:

LIVING SET FREE IN CHRIST

The *Living Set Free in Christ* course manual—as part of the *Living Set Free* course— will help you experience and enjoy the freedom and favor that is found only through Jesus Christ, including topics like: God's original design for your life and His unconditional love for you, how to completely release past hurts and injustices, how to exercise your spiritual authority, how to break the power of spiritual strongholds and generational sin patterns from your life, and much more.

FOUNDATIONS OF FREEDOM

Foundations of Freedom is a five-session experience of the larger *Living Set Free in Christ* course (which is 12 one-hour sessions), and is suitable for use in workshops, small-groups, and one-on-one discipleship settings, as well as for personal devotional use. It provides a primer on starting on a path to freedom in Jesus Christ, equipping you with the biblical truth you need in your pursuit of living the abundant life Jesus promised..

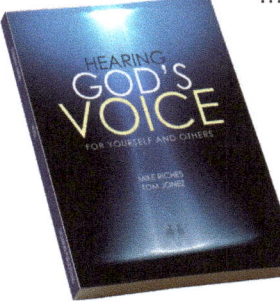

HEARING GOD'S VOICE FOR YOURSELF AND OTHERS

In this illustrated, full-color manual, you'll learn powerful truths and principles for returning to God's biblical normal for communicating with Him. Includes practical assignments for group or class study.

FREEDOM PRAYER TRAINING MANUAL

Freedom prayer ministry is a powerful way to apply the biblical truths of *Living Set Free in Christ* and *Hearing God's Voice*. This training will equip you to help people encounter God's love and truth and be released into the freedom God designed for His children.

Order at www.sycpubglobal.com